The Twin
of the
Christian Life

Effective Prayer and Disciplined Bible Study

by
Dr. Wayne A. Mack
~and~
Joshua Mack

Including selected writings from
J. C. Ryle
Charles H. Spurgeon
Thomas Watson
George Mueller

Grace & Truth Books
Sand Springs, Oklahoma

ISBN# 1-930133-02-2
First printing:
Presbyterian and Reformed Publishing Company, 1977
Second printing, Grace & Truth Books, © 2003

Cover design by Ben Gundersen
Cover photo credit:
Stuart Whatling, London England, with appreciation

Grace & Truth Books
3406 Summit Boulevard
Sand Springs, Oklahoma 74063

Phone: 918 245 1500
www.graceandtruthbooks.com
email: gtbooksoffice@cs.com

TABLE OF CONTENTS

TABLE OF CONTENTS - continued

TABLE OF CONTENTS - continued

Effective Prayer

Introduction

This unit on "Effective Prayer" is designed to help the reader learn how to pray more effectively, that is, in line with the Word of God. It begins with an introductory reading on the prayer habits of George Mueller and continues on with Biblical principles pertaining to prayer. It then moves on to thought-provoking questions, which are designed to lead you into a comprehensive and yet practical study of what the Bible teaches about prayer. Many of the questions are answered in the introductory readings. Some are not. But answers to all questions are found in the Scripture references provided with the questions.

At the conclusion of this unit of our manual, specific suggestions concerning a prayer list, how to pray for missionaries, how to pray for other Christians, sample prayer sheets, and a list of helpful books and tapes are included.

To use this manual in the most profitable way, we recommend that you read the introductory material first and then proceed to the questions. The questions are divided into seven sessions. Each session may be studied one at a time, or, if desired, each session may be broken down into smaller segments.

The Prayer Habits of George Mueller

George Mueller's life stands as a testimony to the power and faithfulness of our Almighty God. Is there someone who doubts whether God still answers prayer? Let them learn from George Mueller. Does anyone doubt whether God is able to accomplish beyond what they could ask or think? Introduce them to George Mueller.

Here is a man who desired to live his life so that "men and women might see that God is faithful still and hears prayer still."[1] By God's grace, that is exactly the kind of life George Mueller lived.

He was born in Prussia in September of 1805. There certainly wasn't anything special about his youth which would make one think that he was going to grow up to be a great man of God. In fact, by looking at his childhood, one would think just the opposite. He wasn't born into a godly home. His father "educated his children on worldly principles."[2] For the first twenty years of his life, George lived an extremely sinful lifestyle. He was a thief. By the age of ten, he was consistently stealing money from his father. He was sent to prison at just sixteen for deception and theft. He stole from his friends and even took money from his pastor. George was not only a thief, he was also a hypocrite. His father sent him to school to train to be a pastor because he knew pastors were paid well. While at school, George studied hard but continued in his sin. He participated in the form of religion, but he had no heart for Christ. "Three or four days before I was confirmed, and thus admitted to partake of the Lord's Supper, I was guilty of gross immorality; and the very day before my confirmation, when I was in the vestry with the clergyman to confess my sins, after a formal manner, I defrauded him..."[3] He would often resolve to live a better life, but to no avail. He didn't care about the Word of God. He writes, "I had no Bible and had not read one for years. I went to church but seldom; but from custom, I took the Lord's Supper twice a year. I had never heard the gospel preached. I had never met with a person who told me that he meant by the help of God, to live according to the Holy Scriptures. In short, I had not the least idea that there were any persons really different from me."[4]

By simply looking at George's youth, many would have assumed he was a hopeless case. Not for God.

Around the age of twenty one, George's life was radically changed. One of his friends took him to a small Bible study held in the home of a true Christian. There he heard the Word preached for the first time and was never the same again. As he walked home after the Bible study had concluded, he remarked to his friend, "All we have seen on our journey to Switzerland, and all our former pleasures, are as nothing in comparison with this evening."[5] He began to love studying the Scriptures and praying. Slowly but surely, he worked at putting off his old sinful practices and putting on righteousness. He developed a great passion for witnessing and had a craving for fellowship with believers.

During this time, God gave George a great desire to be a missionary. Eventually he was sent to London as a missionary to the Jews. After a few years, George became the pastor of a small church. He was wholeheartedly devoted to the authority of Scripture and his preaching and life was a testimony to that. He lived in complete obedience to the Bible and trusted God for his daily needs.

Not too long after his move to England, God led George to establish The Scripture Knowledge Society for the purpose of teaching the lost about God. God used the Society to pass out 2,000,000 Bibles and 111,000,000 tracts, to instruct 121,683 students, and to aid 115 missionaries at a total cost of over one million dollars.

George is most remembered, though, for the orphanages he established. He founded these orphanages for the express purpose of encouraging believers to trust and obey God, no matter what the cost. He wrote, "My spirit longed to be instrumental in strengthening their faith, by giving them not only instances from the Word of God of His willingness and ability to help all those who rely on Him, but to show them by proofs that He is the same in our day."[6] Therefore, he refused to ever ask for money or to let anyone besides God know of his financial needs. Over the course of his life, God provided almost five million dollars for these orphanages which housed over ten thousand orphans.

We can learn a great deal from George Mueller. He was a man of the Word. He dared to be obedient in all that he did. But perhaps we can learn the most from Mueller in the area of prayer. Mueller was a man whose life was saturated with prayer.

Let me just draw seven principles that we can learn from Mueller's example of prayer.

Depend on God Completely

One of the distinguishing marks of George Mueller's life was his absolute reliance upon God for all things. "By the grace of God, I desire that my faith in God should extend towards everything, the smallest of my own temporal and spiritual concerns, and the smallest of the temporal and spiritual concerns of my family, towards the saints among whom I labor, the church at large, etc."[7]

He took all his concerns to God in prayer. Mueller desired to never resolve a problem by leaning upon man or upon human methods, but instead leaned wholly upon God. Thus, he made it a rule never to reveal the financial state of the orphanage to anyone or to ask for funds. (Though we don't have to imitate Mueller in all the specifics of how he did things, we certainly should be challenged by his willingness to depend upon God alone in all things.)

George began his work with the orphans by depending upon God for guidance and strength. His journals make it clear that he continually cried out to God to provide the means to open the orphanage, the staff to run it, and the money to support it. He writes, "So far as I remember, I brought even the most minute circumstances concerning the Orphanage House before the Lord in my petitions, being conscious of my own weakness and ignorance."[8]

He ran the orphanages with an attitude of absolute dependence upon God. Story after story illustrates his humble attitude. For example, in November of 1838 he did not even have a single half-penny to pay for food for any one of the three orphan houses. What did George do? He did not get anxious, but rather took the matter to his Father in prayer. He was confident that God would provide, even though he didn't know how. He began to walk home after praying with his staff, but since he felt he needed exercise, he took the long route. Only twenty yards from his home he met a friend who gave him twenty pounds to meet the orphanage's current needs. Had George been one half minute late, he would have missed him. George always depended upon God, and God always provided.

This attitude gave George great hope and confidence. He writes, "They that trust in the Lord shall never be confounded! Some who helped for a while may fall asleep in Jesus; others may grow cold in the service of the Lord; others may be as desirous as ever to help, but have no longer the means... were we to lean upon man, we should surely be confounded; but, in the leaning upon the living God alone, we are beyond disappointment, and beyond being forsaken because of death, or want of means, or want of love, or because of the claims of other work. How precious to have learned in any measure to stand with God alone in the world, and yet to be happy, and to know that surely no good thing shall be withheld from us whilst we walk uprightly."[9]

George often demonstrated his absolute trust in God. There was one time when a rich man and some of his lady friends were visiting the orphanages. Amazed at the care the orphans were receiving, they looked at George and asked him if he had a large bank account so that he could provide for all these children. George simply answered, "Our funds are deposited in a bank which cannot break." This was quite a statement, as George did not have a penny at the time to provide for the children.[10]

George longed for all believers to depend upon God entirely. He did not want anyone to think that his situation was unique, but instead constantly exhorted Christians to take all their concerns to God in prayer. He often told Christians to make everything a subject of prayer, and to expect answers to requests they have made according to God's will, and in the name of Jesus. We live in a day and age where it is easy to forget our dependence upon God. We have credit cards and our money in bank accounts, and we must never substitute dependence upon human things for dependence upon God. We need to train ourselves to have an attitude of dependence.

Be Specific in Prayer

Mueller brought everything before God in prayer. Too often, due to laziness or lack of faith, many Christians pray only in generalities. They don't want to expect "too much" from God. Mueller's prayer life stands in stark contrast to this kind of attitude.

He prayed to God about financial matters. There were many times when Mueller had not a penny in hand and two thousand children to feed. So he would cry out to God. It is important to note that God took George through many difficult times. We must not get the idea that life was always easy for this man of God. There were times when he cried to God and God immediately answered, and there were other times when he prayed and God took a long time to answer. Yet, he continued to pray. On one occasion, George wanted to buy a certain piece of land on which to build an orphan house. Unfortunately, the owner wanted to sell it at a much greater cost than George could afford. So George went to prayer. He prayed several times a day about this specific matter. After several weeks of prayer, the owner consented to sell the land at the cost George had been praying for.[11]

George cried out to God for physical needs. When he lost a key, he would pray to God to help him find it. When someone did not show up for an appointment, George prayed that he would come quickly.[12] He did not view anything as too small to pray for. There is a simple story which illustrates George's attitude towards prayer requests. One of his favorite young friends once came to him and told him that she wished God would answer her prayers like He did George's. He repeated to her God's promise to listen to His children. So she sat on his knee and he asked her what she wanted to pray for. He prayed with her that God would send her some wool. She ran outside to play, but then realized that she hadn't asked God what kind of wool she wanted. She ran back inside to Mueller.

"I want to pray again."

"Not now, dear, I am busy."

"But I forgot to tell God what color I wanted."

Taking her up on his knee again, Mueller said, "That's right, be definite, my child, now tell God what you want."

That was Mueller's practice in prayer: He was definite, and he told God what he wanted.

Devote Yourself to the Word

There are those who try to separate powerful praying and consistent study of the Scripture. They may say, "I am devoted to prayer, but I have a difficult time studying God's Word." Or perhaps, "I love Scripture, but I am just not into prayer." It really is important to join the two. If we want to be people of prayer, we must be people of the Word; and if we want to truly be people of the Word, we must be people of prayer. Mueller's prayer helped him study the Word and his study of the Word helped him pray.

Mueller emphasized the importance of reading the Scripture prayerfully. He didn't want to come to a passage of Scripture carelessly, but rather continually sought God, asking God to teach him what the passage meant. He often warned against becoming too devoted to Christian books and commentators instead of being devoted to the Scripture and crying out to the Holy Spirit for wisdom.[13]

To Mueller this prayerful reading of Scripture was essential for effective times of prayer. Therefore, Mueller devoted himself to the Word. During the last twenty years of his life, Mueller read the entire Bible approximately four to five times every year. By the end of his life, he had read the entire Bible almost two hundred times. Because he read the Scriptures prayerfully he could pray scripturally. Mueller's study of Scripture was a big part of his success in prayer.

Mueller began to practice this principle early in his Christian life. Before he prayed in the morning he would meditate upon a portion of Scripture. As he would meditate upon Scripture, his soul was drawn to prayer. He would then begin to pray Scripturally. He writes, "... after a very few minutes my soul has been led to confession, or to thanksgiving, or to intercession or to supplication; so that, though I did not, as it were, give myself to prayer, but to meditation, yet it turned out almost immediately more or less into prayer."[14]

Mueller emphasized the importance of the Word of God in prayer for several reasons.

First, praying Scripturally helps the believer develop a proper understanding of who God is and this will strengthen his faith.

As the Christian reads of God's mercy and God's power and sees the wondrous workings of God in the past, he will grow in his faith and thus have greater confidence in the God to whom he prays.[15]

Second, praying Scripturally produces courage during difficult times. When trials come and our circumstances seem difficult we must rest in the promises of God. Mueller wrote, "Further, when sometimes all has been dark, exceedingly dark, with reference to my service among the saints, judging from natural appearances; yea, when I should have been overwhelmed indeed in grief and despair, had I looked at these things after outward appearance; at such times I have sought to encourage myself in God by laying hold in faith of His mighty power, His unchangeable love, and His infinite wisdom... for it is written 'He that spared not His own son, but delivered Him up for us all, how shall He not with Him also freely give us all things?'" Romans 8:32 (KJV).

Thirdly, praying Scripturally informs the believer's prayers. Mueller continually emphasized the importance of not praying according to our own will but according to the will of God. He would often evaluate his prayer requests in light of Scripture in order to make sure that what he was asking was according to God's will. How can we know God's will so we can pray it? We learn God's will through the study of God's Word.

Make Prayer a Priority

It is absolutely impossible to read the life of George Mueller and miss this simple point: George Mueller made prayer a top priority. For Mueller, prayer was not an option, it wasn't something to put on the spiritual back burner—it was his lifeblood.

It's very humbling to read of Mueller's devotion to prayer. His life was saturated with prayer. He prayed privately. He began every day with a time of Scripture reading and prayer. Sometimes these prayer times would last for hours. He would often go for walks with his New Testament and spend time crying out to God. He had a daily time of prayer with his wife. He also scheduled a prayer time with his staff. Yet, this was just the beginning. He prayed continually. When asked if he spent much time on his knees in prayer, Mueller replied, "More or less every day. But I live in the spirit of prayer. I pray as I walk about, when I lie down, when I rise up."[16]

Mueller did not just teach this principle, he lived it. In spite of his preaching schedule, providing care for thousands of orphans, managing a large staff, and taking care of countless details, Mueller always made time for prayer. He explained, "Here is the great secret of success. Work with all your might, but trust not the least in your work . . . pray and then work."[17]

Still others might complain that prayer and study of the Scripture is not enjoyable. Mueller warned against giving in to feelings when it comes to prayer and urged believers to continue to pray and study even when they don't feel like it. One will never develop a desire for prayer and for Scripture unless one works at praying and studying the Scripture.

Mueller would tolerate no excuses for a lack of prayer. We must not regulate prayer to a "last resort" but rather must make it our "first resort."

Keep Christ Central

George Mueller loved Jesus Christ. He recognized that he did not deserve God's grace and that the only reason God answered his prayers was because of the work of Christ. "There is only one thing George Mueller deserves and that is hell. I tell you my brother that is the only thing I deserve. I am indeed a hell-deserving sinner. By nature I am a lost man, but I am a sinner saved by grace."[18]

Therefore, whenever George taught on prayer he always placed great stress upon the absolute necessity of depending upon the "merits and mediation of the Lord Jesus Christ, as the only ground of any claim of blessing."[19] God accepts us not based on our own good works but on the work of His Son. We don't deserve God's grace, and, therefore, we can never become proud when God answers our prayers. We must constantly remind ourselves of our sinfulness and our Savior's mercy.

Mueller challenged believers to meditate deeply on Christ. "Do we seek to ponder what the Lord Jesus Christ is to us, as our Redeemer, as our great High Priest, as the One who is coming again to take us to Himself that where He is we may be also . . . Do we comfort ourselves day by day with all of this?"[20] Christians should constantly be exalting Christ in their prayers and crying out to God on the basis of His work. As one reads through Mueller's prayers it becomes evident that this is exactly what he did. He loved His Savior with all of his heart and clearly worked at exalting Him in his prayers and with His life.

Confess and Forsake Sin

Scripture makes it clear that God does not "listen" to the prayer of the wicked. "He who turns away his ear from listening to the law, even his prayer is an abomination to God" (Proverbs 28:9). Sin hinders our prayers.

I Peter 3:7 illustrates this truth clearly. "You husbands live with your wives in an understanding way, as with a weaker vessel, since she is a woman, and grant her honor as a fellow heir of the grace of life, so that your prayers may not be hindered."

Mueller embraced this principle. He warned "that it is of the utmost importance that we seek to maintain an upright heart and a good conscience, and therefore do not knowingly and habitually indulge in those things which are contrary to the mind of God . . . All my confidence towards God, all my leaning upon Him in the hour of trial will be gone, if I have a guilty conscience and do not seek to put away this guilty conscience but still continue to do the things which are contrary to the will of God."[21] He didn't believe that a Christian should ask God in faith while continuing to indulge unrepentantly in sin.

Confession therefore played an important part in Mueller's prayers. He often asked God to show him his sin and to guard him from making sinful decisions. Mueller sought to mortify his fleshly desires and live solely for Christ. When asked the secret of his success, Mueller replied, "'There was a day when I died, I utterly died,' and as he explained this he bent lower and lower until he almost touched the floor, 'died to George Mueller, his opinions, his preferences, tastes and will - died to the world, its approval, or censure, died to the approval or blame even of my brethren and friend, and since then I have studied only to show myself approved unto God."[22]

Be Persistent in Prayer

One of the most important lessons to be learned from George Mueller's life is how to respond when prayer requests are not quickly answered. For the thousands of Mueller's prayer requests God answered quickly, there were thousands which He delayed in answering. As one reads through Mueller's narratives it is striking how often God made George wait for an answer. How did Mueller respond when God delayed? Through prayer. If God is slow in answering prayer, do not give up. Rather pray more often.

Mueller writes, "One or the other might suppose that all my prayers have been thus promptly answered. No, not all of them. Sometimes I have had to wait weeks, months or years, sometimes many years . . . During the first six weeks of the year 1866 I heard of the conversion of six persons for whom I had been praying a long time. For one I had been praying between two and three years. For another between three and four years; for another above seven years, for the fourth above ten years, for the fifth above fifteen years, and for the sixth above twenty years. In one instance my faith has been tried even more than this. In November 1844, I began to pray for the conversion of five individuals. I prayed every day without one single intermission, whether in sickness or in health, on the land or on the sea, and whatever the pressure of my engagements may be . . . two remain unconverted . . . But I hope in God, I pray on, and I look yet for the answer."[23]

On one of Mueller's many missionary tours, a man who was greatly discouraged came up to him for counsel. This man had six sons for whom he had been praying many years. His sons, in spite of all his prayers, showed no interest in God or their souls. He wanted George to tell him what to do. Mueller simply replied, "Continue to pray for your sons, and expect an answer to your prayers, and you will have to praise God."[24]

When Mueller desired to increase the number of orphans from three hundred to one thousand, he began to pray for God's help in the matter. He kept on praying day after day for eleven years until God answered his prayer.

When Mueller was opening a new home and needed more helpers for the orphan homes, he sought the Lord in prayer. Yet when the home was about to open, he did not have enough applicants to fill the position. How did Mueller respond? By thanking God for previous answered prayers, and deciding not to pray just once a day for this matter, but to pray three times a day for helpers. He did this daily for four months, and was pleased to see God answer his prayers in an incredible way."[25]

Mueller sums up his attitude by simply saying, "When once I am persuaded that a thing is right and for the glory of God, I go on praying until the answer comes. George Mueller never gives up."[26]

Mueller was persistent in prayer for several reasons.

First, he truly believed that God did answer prayer. God's slowness did not shake Mueller's faith. Before Mueller opened his first orphan house he prayed daily for fourteen months and three weeks. "Never, during all these times, had I the least doubt that I should have all that is needed."[27]

Many of us have a difficult time continuing in prayer because in our heart of hearts we aren't sure whether God is really listening to our prayers. Jesus tells us, "What man is there among you, when his son shall ask him for a loaf, will give him a stone. Or if he shall ask for a fish, he will not give him a snake will he. If you then being evil know how to give good gifts to your children, how much more shall your Father who is in heaven give what is good to those who ask Him" (Matthew 7:9-11).

Mueller was confident in this promise and because of that he did not doubt the Father's goodness. "For through grace my mind is so fully assured of the faithfulness of the Lord, that in the midst of the greatest need, I am able to go about my other work. Indeed, if God did not give me this [this confidence in the faithfulness of God] . . . I should scarcely be able to work at all."[28]

Second, he believed that God had good reasons for being slow to answer certain prayers. Mueller could actually rejoice when prayers were not immediately answered because of his complete trust in the wise purposes of God. When God did not immediately answer his prayers, George took it as a sign of His love, because by doing so, God was strengthening Mueller's faith. "Truly it is worth being poor and greatly tried in faith for the sake of having day by day such precious proofs of the loving interest which our kind Father takes in everything that concerns us. And how should our Father do otherwise. He that has given us the greatest possible proof of His love which He could have done, in giving His own Son, surely will He with Him freely give us all things."[29]

Mueller taught that God would often wait to answer prayer in order to strengthen the believer's faith. When a believer's prayers are not answered quickly, rather than trying to take the matter into one's own hands, he should continually look to God for help and wait upon Him for His deliverance. This does not mean that the Christian should do nothing. Mueller believed that a do-nothing attitude was a "counterfeit of faith."[30] Instead the believer should persistently cry out to God and act in obedience to the Scriptures.

Third, Mueller believed that God delighted in His people's earnest prayers. The parable of the widow and the unjust judge gave Mueller great encouragement to continually bring His concerns before His gracious God. God wants His people to pray persistently.

Fourthly, Mueller was persistent in prayer because he longed for the glory of God above all else. "His glory was my chief aim . . . i.e., that it might be seen that it is not a vain thing to trust in the living God."[31] He puts it simply, "The glory of God should always be before the children of God, in what they desire at His hands . . ."[32] The Christian's patience under trial can bring glory and honor to God. Mueller wasn't primarily concerned about Mueller, therefore he was content in all circumstances. He had the attitude of the apostle Paul who said, "Not that I speak from want, for I have learned to be content in all circumstances." Why could Paul say this?

Because Paul was not living for Paul, Paul's life was hidden with Christ, and therefore it did not matter what his life circumstances were like so long as God was glorified. One of the primary reasons many of us have difficulties being persistent in prayer is that we pray with selfish motives. "You ask and you do not receive because you ask with the wrong motives, so that you may spend it on your pleasures" (James 4:3).

A person who is primarily motivated by the glory of God will not become overly discouraged when his prayer requests are not immediately answered. Instead he will rest in the promise of Romans 8:28, "And we know that God causes all things to work together for good to those who love God, to those who are called according to His purpose."

We must follow Mueller's example and continue in prayer even when it is most difficult. "Therefore beloved brethren and sisters, go on waiting upon God, go on praying, only be sure you ask for things which are according to the mind of God . . ."[33]

Power in Prayer

"The effective prayer of a righteous man can accomplish much..." James 5:16-18

God wants us to pray. He makes that abundantly clear. "With all prayer and petition, pray at all times in the Spirit, and with this in mind, be on the alert with all perseverance and petition for all the saints" (Ephesians 6:18). "Pray without ceasing" (1 Thessalonians 5:17). "Let us therefore draw near with confidence to the throne of grace that we may receive mercy and may find grace to help in the time of need" (Hebrews 4:16). God commands us to pray in every circumstance, about everything (Philippians 4:6).

Now those commands are not difficult to understand. But unfortunately for many, they are difficult to obey.

One shouldn't give too much credence to statistics, but I was reading this past week that statistics indicate evangelical Christians by and large pray about three to four minutes a day. I don't doubt that is fairly accurate.

Even the most unreasonable sin attempts to appear reasonable. And so I'm sure there are many reasons believers give for their lack of prayer. The bottom line is that many Christians don't pray because they just don't enjoy it very much. They know they are supposed to pray, but they don't look forward to it. They don't anticipate it. When they do finally pray, they pray with one eye closed and one eye on the clock, wanting to complete this chore so they can get on to a more pleasurable activity.

Perhaps that is how are you are feeling as you begin to read this chapter. Your problem is not knowing that you are supposed to pray; your problem is a lack of desire to do so. Prayer is drudgery for you, a dreaded task. It's like exercising – you know you need to do it, but you wish you didn't have to. But if Scripture were not so clear that you were supposed to pray, you would not do it. Prayer is not refreshing to you. You don't enjoy sweet fellowship with God. You know Christians are supposed to pray, so you pray. That's it. That's the sole reason you do it.

For some of you, the reason you don't enjoy prayer is because you don't really feel you need it. You don't feel desperate for God's help. You are pretty confident in your own ability to handle the situations of life without Him. You know intellectually, at least, what the Scripture says about your need for God, but you don't sense that need in your heart of hearts. So your attitude toward prayer is like that of a teenager who knows he needs to ask his parent's help but really doesn't think he needs it. He grudgingly asks for help. You grudgingly go to prayer to get it over with.

But I'm convinced that is not the only reason some of you may not enjoy prayer the way you should. Many Christians don't enjoy prayer because, although they know what to do, and they know they are supposed to pray, they don't know or aren't convinced why they are to do it. They don't really understand the point of prayer.

Fortunately (and this is one of the things I love about Scripture) God doesn't only show us what to do; He also shows us why.

That's what we find explained in James 5:16-18. Although the preceding verses (13-16a) can be somewhat confusing to understand, the main point is not confusing. James exhorts us to pray. "Is anyone suffering? Let him pray. Is anyone cheerful? Let him sing praises. Is anyone sick? Let him call for the elders … and let them pray … Therefore … *make a habit of* praying for one another." Pray in every circumstance, about everything. That's a command (Philippians 4:6).

But James does not leave it at that. He moves on and seeks to show us why we ought to do so. He does so by making an amazing statement about the nature of prayer and then giving an illustration which proves it.

He writes, "The effective prayer of a righteous man can accomplish much. Elijah was a man with a nature like ours, and he prayed earnestly that it would not rain; and it did not rain on the land for three years and six months. And he prayed again, and the heaven gave rain and the earth produced its fruit."

James is writing to believers who were poor, who were suffering, and who were abused by the rich. They must have felt absolutely powerless. They were refugees living in a foreign country. They weren't powerful people. They definitely didn't have a lot of money. Everything seemed stacked against them.

So he's encouraging them by pointing out that they have hope. They feel like there is nothing they can do. "Well," James says, "you can do something, you can pray." And you should pray, because true prayer is powerful.

The statement he makes about prayer is not really difficult to understand. *The effective prayer of a righteous man can accomplish much.* Prayer is literally a means of power. It "*is effective and it can accomplish much.*" That is a stunning statement.

But (and you need to understand this) James is not simply making a blanket statement about prayer in general. He is very specific.

He uses three different terms for prayer throughout these verses. The first two words, found in verses 13-15, are very general terms for prayer. The particular word he uses for prayer in verse 16, however, is not just another general term. It's very specific. He's not referring to prayer in general, but instead to a very specific kind of prayer. You could translate this word for prayer, "petition," "supplication," or "request." This is the kind of prayer that arises out of a need or a sense of lack. James is talking about a prayer in which you make requests of God. This means he's not just motivating us to pray, but specifically James wants to motivate us to make requests of God in prayer, to go before Him, and to cast our cares upon Him.

Notice he does not simply say, "Prayer can accomplish much ..." Instead he says, "the prayer of a righteous man can accomplish much." This promise, this statement about the power of prayer, applies only to a prayer made by a specific kind of person.

The promise of this verse does not apply to a person who is wicked. There are some who throw out Scripture, because they say, "I prayed and it didn't accomplish anything. Prayer is not effective. It didn't accomplish much for me." But the fact is, God makes quite a *different* promise to those who are living in disobedience to His Word. If you are not a righteous person, God says something completely different about the power and effectiveness of your prayers. He says to those whose prayers are motivated by selfish desires, "You ask and do not receive, because you ask amiss that you may spend it on your pleasures" (James 4:3). Your prayers are not effective because they are motivated by selfish desires. The selfish person can't claim this promise. A man Jesus healed said point blank to those who live in unrepentant sin in John 9:31, "… we know that God does not hear sinners …" If God does not hear a person's prayers, you can be sure that their prayer is not effective, because the power lies not in the prayer itself but in the God who hears the prayer, and God hates the prayers of the unrepentant sinner. The book of Proverbs tells us that "One who turns away his ear from hearing the law, even his prayer is an abomination" (Proverbs 28:9). The prayers of the wicked are not effective and do not accomplish much.

James is not talking about just any prayer. He is talking about the prayers of a righteous man. That term "righteous" indicates to us that he's referring to the prayers of a believer. We know that one of our greatest blessings as believers is that God has credited Christ's righteousness to our account. This means he looks on us and treats us as if we had lived Christ's holy life. As believers there is a sense in which we are all righteous, not because of something we have done but because of what Christ has done. We have confidence that God hears our prayers because we are clothed in the righteousness of Christ.

But I think this little phrase, "the righteous man," implies something more. In the context here, James is speaking of a person who is dealing with his sin in a biblical manner. Look at what he writes immediately before this little statement about the power of prayer. "If you confess your sin and pray for one another you will be healed." Obviously he is not talking then about a person who has never sinned. That is not what he means by the righteous person. But rather he is talking about the person who, although he has sinned and does still sin, seeks to deal with that sin in a godly manner. It is that person's prayers that are effective and will accomplish much.

You see the Bible does teach that even if you are a believer, if you are continuing in unrepentant sin, that sin will affect your prayers. Thomas Watson explains, "Sin lived in makes the heart hard and God's ear deaf. Sin stops the mouth of prayer. It does what the thief does to the traveler – puts a gag in his mouth so that he cannot speak. Sin poisons … prayer. Sin will clip the wings of your prayers so that it will not fly to the throne of grace."[34] If you are living in unrepentant sin you can't expect your prayers to be very effective.

There is a very interesting passage in 1 Peter 3:7 which teaches us just that. Speaking to husbands, Peter says, you must live with your wives in an understanding way so that your prayers will not be hindered. His point is that a failure to obey that command, a failure to live with your wife in the way God desires, will actually hinder the effectiveness of your prayers.

So it's important to understand, before we consider the promise that James makes here, that he is not just talking about any and every kind of prayer. He is very specific. He is speaking about requests made to God by a person who is a believer, who is seeking to obey God, and who, although he is not perfect, is dealing with his sin by repentance and confession on a regular basis. And James promises that that person's prayers, the prayers of a righteous man, are *effective and will accomplish much.*

That's quite a promise. I want you to think about that.

It's obvious that James wants to highlight the power of prayer. That's why he uses two words, not just one. It's as if he can't contain himself. He doesn't merely say that the prayers of a righteous man are effective. He says, the prayers of a righteous man are effective and will accomplish much.

The word effective is a great word. It literally means to have *power to a great degree.*

When you start to look at what God's Word says about prayer you quickly discover that God goes to great lengths to encourage us to pray. And one of the ways he does that is by pointing out to us that prayer is an incredible resource which has great power. Prayer is not a toy, it is a weapon. And it has this power because God promises to hear and answer prayer. In the Psalms, God is called the prayer-hearing God. The Proverbs say that the prayers of the upright are a delight to God. Jesus encourages us to pray by comparing God to a human father, and he says that if a human father who is a sinner loves to take care of his children, how much more will God who is perfect love to listen to, take care of, and answer His children's prayers? Prayer is powerful, not because there is any sort of magic in prayer itself, but because God has promised to hear and answer His children's prayers. So there is a sense in which through prayer you have access to the power and might of God, the Ruler of the Universe.

Charles Spurgeon puts it like this: "… my own soul's conviction is that prayer is the grandest power in the entire universe; that is has a more omnipotent force than electricity, attraction, gravitation, or any of those other secret forces which men have called by names, but which they do not understand. Prayer has a palpable, as true, as sure, as invariable an influence over the entire universe as any of the laws of matter. When a righteous man really prays, it is not a question of whether or not God will hear him; He must hear him – not because there is any compulsion in the prayer, but there is a sweet and blessed compulsion in the promise. God has promised to hear prayer and he will perform his promise. As he is the most high and true God, he cannot deny himself. Oh, to think of this, that you, a puny man, may stand here and speak to God and through God may move all the worlds."[35]

But James doesn't only say prayer is powerful, he says it accomplishes much. That phrase refers *to an ability to get things done.*

Prayer is not merely wishing. It's not an exercise in futility. It's not just talking to the ceiling. True prayer is not simply something we do merely to calm ourselves down. When we go to prayer, we go to work.

You've probably heard of decorative weapons. They are weapons that look like the real thing, but don't work. An actor might use this kind of weapon as a prop in a play. Obviously, there is a great deal of difference between a decorative weapon used in a play by an actor and a weapon used by a soldier in a war.

Prayer is not a decorative weapon. It's not a sword brandied about by an actor in a play. Prayer is an Uzi, a powerful weapon used by a soldier in the midst of a war. It works. As John Piper explains, "Prayer is the walkie-talkie on the battle field of the world. It calls on God for courage (Ephesians 6:19). It calls in for troop deployment and target location (Acts 13:1-3). It calls in for protection and air cover (Matthew 6:13, Luke 21:36). It calls in for firepower to blast open a way for the Word (Colossians 4:3). It calls in for the miracle of healing for the wounded soldiers (James 5:16). It calls in for supplies for the forces (Matthew 6:11, Philippians 4:6). And it calls in for needed reinforcements (Matthew 9:38). This is the place of prayer—on the battlefield of the world. It is a wartime walkie-talkie for spiritual warfare, not a domestic intercom to increase the comforts of the saints. And one of the reasons it malfunctions in the hands of so many Christian soldiers is that they have gone AWOL."[36]

The point is prayer is not fiction. It's not a fantasy. It's not a big long game of make-believe. It's not sitting in a corner in a little orange robe and chanting to yourself. It's reality. Isn't that what James is telling us? Prayer accomplishes things. Prayer gets things done.

Austin Phelps explains, prayer is "one of the most downright, sturdy realities in the universe. Right in the heart of God's plan of government, it is lodged as a power. Amidst the conflicts which are going on in the evolution of that plan, it stands as a power. Into all the intricacies of divine working and the mysteries of divine decree, it reaches out silently as a power. In the mind of God, we may be assured, the conception of prayer is no fiction, whatever man may think of it. It has, and God has determined that it should have a positive and appreciable influence in directing the course of a human life. It is, and God has purposed that it should be, a link of connection between human mind and divine mind, by which through His infinite condescension, we may actually move His will. It is and God has decreed that it should be a power in the universe, as distinct, as real, as natural and as uniform, as the power of gravitation, or of light or of electricity."[37]

Here in James 5:16, it is as if James is taking us to the toolbox. In this toolbox there is a tool that many of us overlook because it doesn't look like much. It looks small and seems insignificant. But James is a master craftsman and he knows his tools. And he realizes that although this little tool might not look like much, it contains great power, it carries a gigantic punch, and it is useful in any and every circumstance. It will help you get things done in a way that no other tool can.

Prayer is effective and it can accomplish much.

Believer, it’s so important that you give prayer its proper place. Truth is often like a narrow path with cliffs on both sides. It’s easy to fall off into error on one side or the other. And that is true when it comes to prayer and understanding what James is talking about.

There are some who might read this chapter and mistakenly think that prayer is like magic—that by prayer I can control God, I can change the mind of God. Hey, James says prayer is effective and can accomplish much!

If that is the power James is talking about, if James is saying that by prayer you can somehow force God to do what you want Him to do, you can be sure, I would not be pleading with you to pray. Because if that were true, prayer would not be a privilege, it would be dangerous. It would be like giving a loaded gun to a little child. I like how one professor puts it, "I will be frank to confess that if I really thought I could change the mind of God by praying, I would abstain. I would have to say, 'How can I presume with the limitations of my own mind and the corruptions of my own heart – how can I presume to interfere in the counsels of the Almighty.' It is almost as if you were to introduce somebody who is utterly ignorant of electronics to a weapons plant in which by pushing certain buttons he could cause an explosion. You say, 'Go ahead and push the buttons. Never mind what happens.' Oh no! There is comfort for the child of God in being assured that our prayers will not change God's mind. This is not what is involved in prayer, and we are not in danger of precipitating explosions by some rash desire on our part."[38] God is not our little genie in a bottle.

When James says there is power in prayer, he is not saying prayer can actually change the mind of God.

But the problem is that others hear that and they go to the opposite extreme. They think, then why pray? I thought you said there was power in prayer? What's the point of praying, if prayer doesn't change things?

Stop there, because if you say that, you've gone too far, you've fallen off the other side of the cliff. Remember how I said you've got to give prayer its proper place? Prayer does not change the mind of God, but prayer does change things. That's what James means when he says prayer is effective and can accomplish much. It is a force, it does do something.

You see, God has established in His Word that prayer is one of the means He uses to accomplish His will here on the earth.

That sounds a little out there, so let me explain.

Suppose I lift my Bible up in the air above my head. I know God is in control of all things, so I can say, "God has ordained that this book should be here in this particular place." He must have ordained it because that is where my Bible is. But, and here's the key, God did not ordain for my Bible to mystically and magically rise in the air all by itself. He ordained that my Bible would rise into the air because I lifted it there.[39]

So God ordained what would happen, and He also ordained how it would happen.

That is the way that God works.

No one, at least no one who is thinking, would say, "why lift your Bible because if God wants it to rise into the air – he will do it without your hand, without you lifting it up." No, we all understand that God uses certain means, like a hand lifting a Bible, to cause things to happen.

And so – this is what you need to understand about prayer – prayer is one of the means God has ordained to cause things to happen.

So you cannot say, why pray, if I do not pray it will happen anyway. That'd be like saying why lift your Bible into the air, if you don't lift your Bible into the air it will happen anyway. No, it will not.

You see that even here in James. Here you've got a guy who is sick, and James doesn't say that God is just going to heal this guy. James says that the elders need to come over and pray and anoint him with oil, and God will raise him up. God used certain means to accomplish the healing. If this man is healed he cannot say that he would have been healed even if he had not prayed. No, because he doesn't know that, and God makes it clear here that there is a means that he is going to use to heal this person, and the means is prayer, verse 15, "the prayer offered in faith will restore the one who is sick …"

Certainly there is a mystery in all this. We cannot fully understand how it all works. But just because we cannot fully understand how it all works does not mean we should start denying that that is how God says it does work. When you turn on a light, most of us do not fully understand all that is happening there, but just because we do not fully understand it does not mean we do not do it. Or when you pick up a phone, most of us do not fully understand how our voice can get all the way across the country in an instant, but that does not mean we stop picking up the phone. So we may not fully understand how prayer works, but we know God says it does, and so we have faith in that, and we keep turning on the light switch, we keep picking up the phone, we keep praying, because we know God knows more than we do. And He has said that prayer is one of the primary means He uses to accomplish His will.

You look at Scripture and you see that prayer is one of the means God has used to deliver His people, to rescue them. You remember the book of Exodus, which is the story of Israel's great escape from Egypt. God does some amazing things in that book. It is interesting to note where it all started. Back in Exodus 2, Israel is enslaved in Egypt. They are being persecuted mercilessly. And there are two neat little verses in chapter 2, verses 23 and 24, "Now it came about in those days that the king of Egypt died. And the sons of Israel sighed because of their bondage and they cried out; and their cry for help because of their bondage rose up to God. So God heard their groanings; and God remembered His covenant with Abraham, Isaac, and Jacob. And God saw the sons of Israel, and God took notice of them." God stepped in to deliver His people because His people through prayer reminded Him of His promise.

Or how about Jonah? Jonah is in the belly of a whale. How do you get out of that? He says in Jonah 2, "I called out of my distress to the Lord, and He answered me. I cried for help from the depth of Sheol, and Thou didst hear my voice."

Prayer is one of the means God has used to provide physical blessings to His people. I think especially of Hannah in 1 Samuel 1. She is so sad because she's unable to have children. So she goes to the temple and she just cries out to God in prayer. God hears her prayer, and she has a child. She explains how this happened in verse 27, "For this boy I prayed, and the Lord has given me my petition which I have asked of Him." Why did Hannah have this child? She says it was because God heard her prayer.

Prayer is one of the means God has used to provide spiritual blessings to His people. Cornelius in the book of Acts 10 is a good example of this. He was a devout man, but he did not know all he needed to know. He had an inadequate understanding of God. Nonetheless, he was devoted to prayer, and God heard his prayers. God sent Peter to proclaim the gospel to him. Do you know why? An angel said, "Cornelius your prayer has been heard and your alms have been remembered before God" (Acts 10:31). By the way, I think that is a good answer to those who say, "What about those people out there that don't have the gospel?" If they, like Cornelius, are truly seeking God and crying out to Him, God hears their prayers.

If you want to know what prayer can accomplish, Paul is a good real-life illustration. He is constantly pointing out the power of prayer. For one, when you observe most of his letters, you notice that he begins, "Look I'm constantly praying for you." Praying for what? Spiritual fruit, growth in love, change. Obviously, Paul wouldn't do that, if he didn't think prayer worked. And you will also notice that he is always saying, "I thank God for this or that in your life." Why does he thank God? Because he knows that the change in their lives was due to God's work in their hearts. Sometimes I get discouraged when I look at my life or I talk to people, because the truth is, people by themselves do not really seem to change all that much. You know you are stuck in the same habits for a long time or you talk to people and they are stuck in the same habits for a long period of time, and you wonder what you can do. Well, there is hope. Because God does hear our prayers, and He does answer them, and He is able to truly transform someone from the inside out. When you read Paul's prayers, you see that.

Paul points out another thing he believes prayer is able to do. He says in Colossians 4:3, "pray for us, that God may open up to us a door for the word, that we may speak forth the mystery of Christ ..." Paul is saying prayer can accomplish something here. God can use prayer to open up opportunities to share the gospel. He says in 2 Thessalonians 3:1, "Pray for us that the word of the Lord may spread rapidly and be glorified, just as it did also with you." If you want the word of God to spread, to be glorified, what you need to do is pray, because God can use prayer to do just that.

We must never minimize the importance of prayer. When we pray our voices are heard in heaven.

James knows we might be tempted to minimize the power of prayer, so he gives us a striking illustration in 5:17-18 to prove his point.

"Elijah was a man with a nature like ours, and he prayed earnestly that it might not rain; and it did not rain on the earth for three years and six months. And he prayed again, and the sky poured rain, and the earth produced its fruit."

For those of you who do not think prayer can accomplish much, for those of you who feel hopeless and feel like all is lost, you need to remember Elijah.

Elijah prayed. God heard his prayers. And it stopped raining. For three and a half years. Then he prayed again. And it started raining.

Do you get that?

If James is saying anything, he is saying that God can use one man's prayers to accomplish big, great, huge things, like controlling even nature.

But you say, "Hey I'm not Elijah. I'm nobody important like that."

You can't look at this illustration and say that was just Elijah because James' whole point is to say that wasn't just Elijah. That's why he makes it clear, "Elijah was a man just like us."

We serve the same God Elijah did. He is just as powerful today. And we have the same weapon at our disposal, the weapon of prayer.

Recently God allowed me to participate in the planting of a church. It was a real struggle. Honestly, I never had too much of a problem thinking I could really start the church and make the church work by myself. I knew I could not do it. My problem was a bit different. There were moments when I lost hope. Felt like there was nothing I could do. Almost became fatalistic. Now it's fine to understand that there's nothing you can do, but it is not fine to lose hope, because there is hope. It is right here in James 5:16. God answers prayer.

Humility is good; hopelessness is not. There is a difference between true humility and hopelessness. It is not humble to be fatalistic. It is unbelief. You are not just saying something about yourself, you are saying something about God. You do not think He answers prayer. Humility turns you to God in prayer, because you realize that although you cannot do anything, God can, and you realize that prayer is the means God has ordained for accomplishing His great purpose.

There is an old allegory cited by Charles Spurgeon that illustrates this:

> "Once upon a time, the king of Jerusalem left his city in the custody of an eminent Captain, whose name was Zeal. He gave to Zeal many choice warriors, to assist him in the protection of the city. Zeal was a right hearted man, one who never wearied in the day of battle, but would fight all day, and all night, even though his sword did cleave to his hand as the blood ran down his arm. But it happened upon this time, that the king of Arabia, getting unto himself exceeding great hosts and armies, surrounded the city, and prevented any introduction of food for the soldiers, or of

ammunition to support the war. Driven to the last extremity, Captain Zeal called a council of war, and asked them what course they should take. Many things were proposed, but they all failed to effect the purpose, and they came to the sad conclusion that nothing was before them but the surrender of the city, although upon the hardest terms.

Zeal took the resolution of the council of war, but when he read it, he could not bear it. His soul abhorred it. "Better" he said "to be cut in pieces than to surrender. Better for us to be destroyed while we are faithful than to give up the keys of this royal city." In his great distress, he met a friend of his, called Prayer, and Prayer said to him, "Oh! Captain I can deliver this city." Now, Prayer was not a soldier, at least he did not look as if he were a warrior, for he wore the garments of a priest. In fact he was the king's chaplain, and was a priest of the holy city of Jerusalem. But nevertheless Prayer was a valiant man and wore armor beneath his robes. "Oh! Captain," said he, "give me three companions and I will deliver this city – their names must be Sincerity, Importunity, and Faith." Now these four brave men went out of the city at the dead of night when the prospects of Jerusalem were the very blackest, they cut their way right through the hosts that surrounded the city. With many wounds and much smuggling they made their escape, and traveled all night long as quickly as they could across the plain, to reach the camp of the king of Jerusalem. When they flagged a little, Importunity would hasten them on; and when at any time they grew faint, Faith would give them a drink from his bottle, and they would recover. They came at last to the palace of the great king, the door was shut, but Importunity knocked long, and at last it was opened.

> Sincerity threw himself on his face before the throne of the great king and Prayer began to speak. He told the king of the great straits in which the beloved city was now placed, the dangers surrounding it, and the almost certainty that all the brave warriors would be cut in pieces by the morrow. Importunity repeated again and again the wants of the city, Faith pleaded hard the royal promise and the covenant. At last the king said to Captain Prayer, "Take with thee soldiers and go back, lo I am with Thee to deliver this city."
>
> At morning light, just when the day broke for they had returned more swiftly than could have been expected, for though the journey seemed long in going there it was short in coming back, in fact they seemed to have gained time on the road, they arrived early in the morning, fell upon the hosts of the king of Arabia, took him prisoner, defeated his army, divided the spoil, and entered the gates of Jerusalem in triumph. Zeal put a crown of gold upon the head of Prayer, and decreed henceforth that whenever Zeal went forth to battle, Prayer should be the standard bearer, and should lead the army into the fray."[40]

Prayer is effective. It accomplishes much.

I want to close by asking you a very simple question: Do you believe that? Or do you say to yourself, "This is all great. Sounds nice in church. We've all heard it before."

But let me just ask you: Do you really believe in prayer? Do you really believe that prayer is mighty in what it is able to do? As Charles Spurgeon wrote, "I know you pray because you are God's people; but do you believe in the power of prayer? There are a great many Christians that do not, they think it is a good thing, and they believe that sometimes it does wonders, but they do not think that prayer, real prayer is always successful…"

I want prayer to be a joy for you. I want it to be a thrill. If you really believe what James teaches here, it will be a joy. It will be a thrill.

I like how one old writer has put it. If you truly believe James 5:16, "the feeling which will become spontaneous with a Christian under the influence of such a trust, is this, 'I come to my devotions this morning on an errand of real life. This is no romance and no farce. I do not come here to go through a form of words. I have no hopeless desires to express. I have an object to gain. I have an end to accomplish. This is a business in which I am about to engage. An astronomer does not turn his telescope to the skies with a more reasonable hope of penetrating those distant heavens than I have of reaching the mind of God by lifting up my heart to the throne of grace. This is the privilege of my calling of God in Christ Jesus. Even my faltering voice is to be now heard in heaven, and it is to put forth a power there, the results of only which God can know and eternity can develop. 'Therefore O Lord, thy servant findeth it in his heart to pray this prayer unto thee.'''[41]

Paul Teaches Us How to Pray

In Luke 11:1 the disciples of our Lord came to Him and said, "Lord, teach us to pray." These disciples sensed the inadequacy of their own prayer life and came to Jesus for instruction. I am sure that every true Christian has a feeling of inadequacy when it comes to the matter of prayer. I confess that though I believe I have been a Christian for more than twenty years, I still feel that I am just a child in this matter of prayer. I confess that there are times when I have almost envied the disciples and wished that I could come into the physical presence of Jesus Christ to ask my Lord to teach me to pray. While I have felt this way, I realize that this feeling is wrong, because we have advantages and privileges that these disciples did not have. We have a fuller understanding and experience of the Holy Spirit than they had. We have the entire New Testament of which they had none when they approached our Lord in Luke 11.

In the Bible, according to 2 Timothy 3:16-17, God has given us everything that we need to make us complete and thoroughly equipped unto every good work. Certainly one of the works to which the Bible equips us is this work of prayer. In the Bible we have the example and the teachings of our Lord Jesus Christ concerning prayer, and we have the examples and teachings of the inspired apostles of our Lord Jesus Christ concerning prayer. Perhaps the reason that many of us feel such a sense of inadequacy in our own prayer lives is because either we are not studying what the Bible has to say about prayer, or we are not applying what the Bible has to say about prayer to our own experience.

To help us to know better how to pray, let us examine one of the many prayers of the apostle Paul which are found in the Bible. In Ephesians 1:15-19 we read, "Wherefore I also, after I heard of your faith in the Lord Jesus, and love unto all the saints, cease not to give thanks for you, making mention of you in my prayers; that the God of our Lord Jesus

Christ, the Father of Glory, may give unto you the spirit of wisdom and revelation in the knowledge of Him: The eyes of your understanding being enlightened; that ye may know what is the hope of His calling, and what the riches of the glory of His inheritance in the saints, and what is the exceeding greatness of His power to usward who believe, according to the working of His mighty power."

Certainly Paul was one of the greatest Christians the world has ever known. Paul was not simply a great preacher. He was not simply a great theologian. Even more important, he was a great Christian. Even if he had not been a great theologian or a great preacher, Paul still would have been a great person because he was a great Christian. Assuredly one of the things that made Paul the great Christian that he was was his prayer life.

Let us notice several facts about Paul's prayer life in Ephesians 1:15-19. *First, notice the person to whom Paul prayed. Paul did not address his prayers to a departed saint.* Paul did not pray, "Oh, father Abraham," or "Oh, prophet Isaiah," or "Oh, saint so and so." In the Bible there is only one example of anyone praying to a departed saint. That is found in Luke 16:24. It is significant to notice where this man was when he prayed that prayer; he was in hell. It is also significant to notice that this prayer was never answered. The rich man in hell lifted up his voice and he cried, "Father Abraham." He prayed to a departed saint. He said, "Send Lazarus with some water that he may cool my tongue." Abraham said, "Nothing doing. I cannot do it." The only prayer addressed to a departed saint in the Bible was not answered. The Bible teaches us very clearly that it is a foolish thing for us to worship or pray to saints of God. When Cornelius fell down in the presence of Peter in Acts 10, Peter said, "Get up off your face. I am just a man like you are."

Furthermore, *Paul did not pray to some vague, indistinct, abstract spirit in the sky.* He did not make his prayer to "the man upstairs." He did not address "somebody bigger than you and me." He did not address his prayer to God, "whoever you are and wherever you are, somewhere out there, hear me when I cry." Nor did he pray to the god of Buddha, or the god of Confucius, or to the god of Mohammed, or the God of all men. No, *he addressed his prayer to the God of our Lord Jesus Christ, the Father of glory.*

When *the apostle Paul prayed to the God of our Lord Jesus Christ,* he meant that he was praying to *the God whom our Lord Jesus Christ had revealed.* The Scriptures say, "The Word was made flesh [referring to Jesus Christ] and dwelt among us, (and we beheld his glory, the glory as of the only begotten of the Father,) full of grace and truth" (John 1:14). The Bible says in John 1:18, "No man has seen God at any time; the only begotten God, who is in the bosom of the Father, He has explained Him." In John 14:9 Jesus said, "He that hath seen me hath seen the Father." In Hebrews 1:3 we read that He is "the express image of His person." Paul is praying to that personal God, that holy God, that gracious God, that merciful God, that omnipotent God, that sovereign God, whom Jesus Christ came to reveal. There is some content in those words that Paul used when he said, "Oh, God of our Lord Jesus Christ."

When Paul prayed to the God of our Lord Jesus Christ in Ephesians 1:17, he also meant that *he was coming to God only on the basis of Jesus Christ.* He realized that the only basis on which he as a sinner could approach a holy God was through the one mediator that God had provided between God and men, even that man Christ Jesus. The Bible says, "For there is one mediator between God and men, the man Christ Jesus." Paul knew that Jesus Christ is the way, the truth, and the life; and that no man cometh unto the Father but by Him. Paul tells us in Ephesians 2:18 that it is by Jesus Christ that we have access unto the Father. As he approaches God in prayer, he does not say, "Lord, remember what I have done for you; Lord, remember how righteous I have been." No, he pleads the merit; he pleads the person of Jesus Christ. He reminds God of Jesus Christ. Of course, this is the only proper approach in prayer. We dare come to a holy God only through Jesus Christ. According to 1 Peter 2:5, our spiritual sacrifices are acceptable to God only through Jesus Christ. Paul came knowing that the golden key that unlocks the door into the presence of God is the person of Jesus Christ. As Paul came, he prayed to the God of our Lord Jesus Christ.

He also prayed to the God who was the Father of glory. Thomas Goodwin says that this may mean that Paul was praying to the Father who was glorious. It may mean that he was saying, "Thou art the glorious Father." Now *God the Father is the glorious Father. He is the majestic God.* The Scriptures say, "The heavens declare the glory of God; and the firmament sheweth forth his handiwork" (Psalm 19:1). The Scriptures say, "Oh, Lord our Lord, how excellent is thy name in all the earth! Who hast set thy glory above the heavens." The Scriptures tell us that our God is in the heavens and that He is majestic. When Isaiah saw Him, the angels were singing of Him, "Holy, holy, holy is the Lord of hosts; the whole earth is full of His glory." Isaiah saw the glory of God and he had to fall on his face. Moses said, "Lord, show me your glory." God said, "I cannot Moses, or you will die. Go back there in the cleft of the rock and I will let you see a little bit of my glory. You'd better be careful because if you see my entire glory, you will die." Our God is a glorious God. Paul may be reminding the Father and himself about this when he comes in prayer. Thomas Goodwin also suggests that when Paul used the phrase, "the Father of glory," he may be addressing God as the one who is the source of glory. All glory comes from God. God created the glory of the heavens. And God bestows on us, according to Psalm 84:11, ''grace and glory.'' The Scriptures say that ''the sufferings of this present time are not worthy to be compared with the glory which shall be revealed" (Romans 8:18). Colossians 3:4 says, "When Christ, who is our life, shall appear, then shall ye also appear with him in glory." In Romans 5:2 Paul says, "We rejoice in the hope of the glory of God." God bestows glory upon us; the glory of fellowship with Himself; the glory of forgiveness; the glory of renewed bodies; and eventually, of course, the glory of heaven. Paul came to God and he said, "Oh, Thou art the glorious Father; Thou art the source of all glory. Lord, bestow some of your abundance upon us."

Secondly, notice not only the person to whom Paul prayed but the people for whom Paul prayed. In Ephesians 1:15 Paul says, "Wherefore I also, after I heard of your faith in the Lord Jesus, and love unto all the saints." The people for whom Paul prayed were *people that he had heard about.* Acts 19 tells us that Paul was the one whom God used to found the church at Ephesus. Yet here he says that he was praying for people that he had heard about. What did he mean? Well, you must remember that Paul had not seen these people for several years. He was in prison when he wrote this epistle. Apparently Paul had recently received new information about these Christians at Ephesus. This new information had stimulated him to pray for them even more. Here we see Paul praying for people that he had not seen for some time, people that he was not in constant association with, people that he had simply heard about. Paul tried to keep aware of what was happening in the churches he had founded.

In 1 Thessalonians 3:5-10 Paul says, "For this cause, when I could no longer forbear [I could not wait any longer] I sent to know your faith [he was like a mother whose children had been away for a period of time; he was anxious and concerned about them for he had not heard anything about them for awhile and could not wait any longer; so he sent a messenger to find out how they were] lest by some means the tempter had tempted you, and our labour be in vain. But now when Timotheus came from you unto us, and brought us good tidings of your faith and charity, and that ye have good remembrance of us always, desiring greatly to see us, as we also to see you: Therefore, brethren, we were comforted over you in all our affliction and distress by your faith: For now we live, if ye stand fast in the Lord. [Paul says that if you are standing fast in the Lord, I live; I am happy; I rejoice.] For what thanks can we render to God again for you, for all the joy wherewith we joy for your sakes before our God [Paul says, 'If you only knew how happy you make me and how you stir me up to give thanks unto God when I hear good reports about you."]; Night and day praying exceedingly that we might see your face, and might perfect that which is lacking in your faith?" And then he continues praying for these Thessalonians. When he heard about them, he went to prayer. He was not with them in person. He was not constantly seeing them, and yet Paul did not forget to pray for those about whom he heard.

But this word "heard" probably indicates more than the fact that Paul was praying for those whom he had known previously and now had heard something new about. It probably indicates that there were some new people in the church at Ephesus that Paul had never met personally. The church was a growing church. Paul heard about new converts in the church at Ephesus. He only knew about them by report and yet Paul was moved to pray for them. This should teach us something about our prayer lives. It should teach us that *we should not only pray for the people in our own assembly that we see week after week and day after day.* It should teach us that we as prayer warriors should be praying for others that we only hear about. Certainly Paul is not saying that we should not be praying for those that we see constantly. But we very seldom forget to pray for those that we see regularly. We do not forget to pray for our families, because we are confronted by our families constantly. We do not forget to pray for each other because we see each other constantly. But the people that we are most apt to forget to pray for are those that we do not see frequently or those that we have never seen. Paul teaches us that we ought to pray for people that we only hear about as well as for people we see often.

But still further, notice that the people for whom Paul prayed were *people who were in a spiritually prosperous condition.* Paul said, "Wherefore I also, after I heard of *your faith* in the Lord Jesus, and *love unto all the saints"* went to prayer for you. These people were spiritually prosperous. They were people who had faith in our Lord Jesus Christ.

They were not walking by sight; they were walking by faith. We can define faith by making an acrostic out of the word. Faith is forsaking all I trust Him. Forsaking all confidence in myself, I trust Christ. Forsaking all confidence in my good works, I trust Christ for salvation. Forsaking all confidence in my own abilities to supply my needs, I trust Christ to supply my needs. Forsaking all confidence in myself to handle the future, I trust Christ concerning the future. Here were people who were trusting Christ. They were walking by faith. They were living by faith. They were not worrying; they were not falling apart; but walking confidently forward, trusting the Lord Jesus Christ.

Not only were they people who had faith, they were people who were manifesting love unto all the saints. They were manifesting their love to the weak saints, to the prudish saints, to the extroverted saints, to the introverted saints. They were manifesting their love to the rich saints, to the poor saints, to the little-faith saints, to the stubborn saints, to the moody saints, to all kinds of saints. They did not have little cliques in the church at Ephesus. They did not say, "Look, you have got to be just like me or I will not love you." No, there was real love among the people. It was one big family. They were one body in Christ. There were not any parties and factions as there were in the church in Corinth. Paul could write and say, "I see that you are loving all the saints. I have heard about this."

What does it mean in practical terms to love the saints? What was happening in the church at Ephesus? First Peter 4:8-9 tells us what it means in practical terms to love the saints. We read, "And above all things have fervent love among yourselves: for love shall cover the multitude of sins. Use hospitality one to another without grudging." These Ephesian Christians were covering a multitude of sins. They were using their homes and everything that they had to serve the rest of the people of God. To love the brethren as these people were means, according to Galatians 6:1-2, that they were bearing one another's burdens and so fulfilling the law of Christ. What was the law of Christ that they were to fulfill? It was the law laid down in John 13:34-35, where Jesus said, "A new commandment I give unto you, That ye love one another; as I have loved you, that ye also love one another. By this shall all men know that ye are my disciples, if ye have love one to another."

Do you know what Galatians 6:2 really means when it says, "Bear ye one another's burdens"? Sometimes we think it means that if someone is carrying a great big hundred-pound-weight bag, we go over and lift the bag and carry it for them. That is not what the word burden there means. You have to take it in its context and interpret it in connection with verse 1. Galatians 6:1 says, "Brethren, if a man be overtaken in a fault, ye which are spiritual, restore such an one in the spirit of meekness; considering thyself, lest thou also be tempted." Bear one another's what? Concerns. Bear one another's weaknesses. Bear one another's problems. What he is saying is, "Put up with the infirmities and weaknesses of the saints. Try to get rid of their infirmities and their weaknesses." This is how you show love one to another. This is the kind of love that the people of God at Ephesus were manifesting one toward another. And yet Paul tells them, I am praying for you. Why, Paul? Why waste your time? Why pray for these people? You ought to be praying for someone else who is more needy. These people were spiritually prosperous and yet Paul was praying for them.

Let me ask you. Who are the people that you really pray for? The spiritually prosperous people? I challenge you to check the epistles of the apostle Paul and find out how often he tells spiritually prosperous people he is praying for them. He did not take them off his prayer list when they were doing well in the things of God. *He prayed for spiritually prosperous people. Why?*

First of all, because *there is always room for growth.* As long as we are in this world, no Christian has arrived at perfection. We trust Christ but we do not trust Christ as much as we should. We love the saints but we do not love the saints as much as we should. We serve Christ, but we do not serve Christ as much as we should. We know something of the Word of God but none of us knows as much of the Word of God as we ought to know of the Word of God. No church is as spiritual as it could be. There is no church which is so spiritual that it does not need our prayers and that it cannot make progress. Dear ones, there is a terrible danger when we see God beginning to bless to slack off in our prayers. Do you know anything about that danger? We pray when the problems and difficulties are there. Then all of a sudden when we see the problem behind us, we begin to slack off; we begin to fall back. We stop pressing on quite as zealously as we did before.

I remember when I was playing football in high school. We were unbeaten in the last nine games of my sophomore year and all the games in my junior year. We came into my senior year and won the first seven or eight games. We had run up one of the longest unbeaten streaks of any football team in Pennsylvania at that particular time. We fellows on the football team (some of us had played together for three years) began to get a little cocky. We thought that we did not have to practice as hard. We began to feel that when we went out on the field the other teams would know our record and just roll over and play dead. But it did not work that way, because even teams that are winning need to make progress or else they are going to be defeated. They need to continue to persevere. Do you know what happened? We lost the last two games of my senior year to teams that were beaten by teams that we had beaten badly, because we had a letdown. I believe that the same thing often happens among the people of God. We see God giving us a measure of blessing so we slow down instead of pressing on. Paul knew that, so he said, "I know that you are going well, but there is always room for growth. I am going to pray for you."

Secondly, Paul also knew *the terrible danger of backsliding.* Paul knew that spiritually prosperous Christians can backslide. He knew that spiritually prosperous churches can become barren churches. He had some experience of that in his own associations. In Philemon 24 he writes of Demas, who was his fellow laborer. Just a bit later he writes in 2 Timothy 4:10 of Demas "who hath forsaken me, having loved this present world." I know of professing Christians who were once apparently strong in faith, who had a tremendous love for the brethren. They have now left their first love and are no longer walking with Christ as they once were. I know of churches where there was love, fidelity, zeal, and commitment for Christ, which have now lost that first love, that zeal, that enthusiasm, that fidelity and commitment. Sometimes the doctrine, sometimes the orthodoxy is still there, but there is something missing. What has happened? They have left their first love.

The church at Ephesus itself stands as a terrible warning of this possibility. In Ephesians 1:15, when Paul writes to them, he tells them, "I know of your faith in our Lord Jesus Christ, and your love to all the saints." Yet some thirty years later, when the Lord Jesus spoke to this church in Revelation 2:4-5a, do you know what he said to them? He said, "Nevertheless I have somewhat against you, because you have left your first love. Remember from whence thou art fallen."

This fact ought to cause us to pray earnestly for churches that are now in a spiritually prosperous condition. They can lose their enthusiasm. They can lose their zeal. They can lose their commitment to Jesus Christ and truth. We need to continue to pray for ourselves and for others, even if we are now spiritually healthy, because of the terrible danger of backsliding. All of us have been in churches where there have been coldness and deadness, and we come away saying,

"Thank God for what we have in our church." But our church could become just like these other churches if we do not pray and press on. Let us then learn from Paul something about the people for whom we should pray.

Thirdly, let us notice the main emphasis of Paul's praying. In the thirteen epistles of Paul there are more than twenty recorded prayers. An examination of these prayers reveals that *Paul was mainly concerned about spiritual matters when he prayed for people.* You never find it recorded that he prayed for Aunt Susie's sore big toe. You never find that he prayed for someone's stomachache. You read through these epistles and the burden of his prayer was for their spiritual condition. Look at what he prays for here in Ephesians 1. He prays in verses 17-18 "that God might give the spirit of wisdom and revelation in the knowledge of him, that the eyes of your understanding might be enlightened so that ye may know what is the hope of his calling, and what the riches of the glory of his inheritance in the saints, and what is the exceeding greatness of his power to usward who believe." Or read his prayer for the Philippians in Philippians 1:9-11. It is the same. He prays that their love might abound in all judgment and knowledge; that they might be given the ability to discern that which is excellent and that they might be sincere and without offense until the day of Jesus Christ and that they might be filled with the fruits of righteousness, which are by Jesus Christ unto the glory and praise of God. When he prayed for the Colossians he asked that they might be filled with the knowledge of His will, that they might walk worthy of the Lord unto all pleasing, that they might be fruitful unto every good work, that they might increase in the knowledge of God, that they might be strengthened with His mighty power unto all joyfulness, and patience, and longsuffering. *The main emphasis of Paul's prayers was spiritual. In praying as well as in living, Paul sought first the kingdom of God and His righteousness.*

This was true when he prayed for others and this was also true when he asked others to pray for him. Where was

Paul when he wrote the Ephesian epistle? He was languishing in a Roman prison. If you had been languishing in a Roman prison for the years that Paul had been there, what would you have asked the Ephesians to pray for you? Let us see what Paul asked them to pray about in Ephesians 6:18-20. As we look at this, I think many of us can see the shallowness of our prayer lives and of our commitment to Jesus Christ. We can see that in many ways we get our sense of values completely distorted. We spend more time praying about things that are of lesser importance than we do about things that are of major importance. Paul says in Ephesians 6:18-20, "Praying always with all prayer and supplication in the Spirit, and watching thereunto with all perseverance and supplication for all saints; And for me that utterance may be given unto me, that I may open my mouth boldly, to make known the mystery of the gospel, For which I am an ambassador in bonds: that therein I may speak boldly, as I ought to speak." He did not say, "Oh, Brethren, pray for me that Caesar might take a liking to me and release me from prison." He says, "Just pray that right here where I am I will be bold to preach the gospel. Pray that I will take every opportunity I have to make known the mystery of the gospel." He did not say, "Pray that God will get me released from this situation." He said, "Oh, Ephesian Brethren, pray for me that right here in this situation, I will be the kind of Christian, the kind of witness that I ought to be." He did the same thing when he wrote to the Colossians. In Colossians 4:3 he says, "Withal praying also for us, that God would open unto us a door of utterance, to speak the mystery of Christ, for which I am also in bonds." In this emphasis on the spiritual the apostle Paul was following the example of our Lord. When our Lord prayed for his disciples in John 17 he did not pray for anything physical. Everything he prayed for was spiritual.

At this point I want to put in a word of caution so that I won't be misunderstood. I am not saying that Paul never prayed for material things. I am not saying that he never asked other people to pray for him about material things. In

Philippians 4:6 he said, "Be anxious for nothing; but in every thing by prayer and supplication with thanksgiving let your requests be made known unto God." It would seem to me that the "everything" would include the physical and material things. But what I am saying is that Paul was more concerned about spiritual matters than he was about the physical and material. It showed up in the burden of his prayers for others as well as in the prayer requests that he sent to other people for himself. This demonstrated the fact that Paul was a man who sought first the kingdom of God and His righteousness.

I say, let us examine our prayer lives. Let us examine our prayer meetings. What is the burden of our praying? Does our praying reveal that we are most concerned about people's souls and their spiritual condition or that we are most concerned about their physical condition? I am not saying that we should not pray for their physical and material condition. Jesus did say that we should pray, "Give us this day our daily bread." But remember that he only taught us to pray one request for daily bread and many other requests for spiritual needs. In our praying our main concern ought to be for the spiritual needs and spiritual conditions of people, because, after all, a man may have a good body and die and go to hell. It is his soul that is most important. Let us keep that in view as we pray for one another and as we pray for our churches. It is fine for us to pray for good physical facilities, and we ought to be concerned about that; but more than physical facilities in which the church meets, let us pray for the church itself and for the spiritual condition of the people who make up the church.

Fourthly, we note that Paul's praying included thanksgiving. Paul tells the Ephesian Christians in verse 1:16, "I cease not to give thanks for you." As you read his other epistles, you will find him saying again and again that he is giving thanks. In Philippians 4:6 he said that we are to make our requests known unto God with thanksgiving. In 1 Timothy 2:1 he said that we are to give thanks for all men. In

Colossians 4:2 he said, "Continue in prayer and watch in the same with thanksgiving." Paul practiced what he preached. He not only told others to give thanks in their prayers, he gave thanks in *his* prayers. Paul said, "Give thanks for all things." "In everything give thanks" (1 Thessalonians 5:18).

As I went through the prayers of the apostle Paul, I noticed one specific thing for which Paul thanked God again and again. In almost every epistle that he wrote, *he thanked God for the people of God.* He thanked God for the saints. In Romans 1:8, he says, "First, I thank my God through Jesus Christ for you all." (The first thing that I am thanking God for is you Christians.) He did the same thing in Ephesians, 1 Corinthians, Philippians, Colossians, 1 and 2 Thessalonians, 2 Timothy, and Philemon. Paul appreciated God's people. He knew that he could not get along without them. Thus in his prayers he often had to say, "Thank you, Lord, for Christian brethren." Paul really loved the people of God. Do we love the people of God? Do we really appreciate the people of God? Let us examine our prayer lives to find out.

There are two things that Paul often thanked God for about other Christians. *One was their faith.* In his epistles, he did not thank God that they had such nice personalities, or that they had many talents, or such great resources, or that they were able to give much to the church, or that they had good jobs. No, Paul said, "I want to thank you, Lord, for their faith." In Romans 1:8 he said, "I thank thee, Lord, that their faith is spoken of throughout the whole world." He did this in Thessalonians and then again in Philemon. Paul knew where that faith came from. Faith is a gift of God. He said, "I thank God for the fact that you have faith because it is God who has given you that faith." *Secondly, Paul often thanked God for their love to all the saints, because the fruit of the Spirit is love* (Galatians 5:22). They did not pump this love up in themselves. They got it from God. Paul let them know that he was thanking God for the spiritual qualities found in their lives.

But he not only thanked God for these spiritual qualities, *he let these Christians know that he saw the spiritual qualities in their lives, He let them know that he appreciated them.* Do we do that? First of all we ought to thank God, and then we ought to encourage one another. When some brother is growing in grace and becoming a challenge to us, we ought to go to that brother and tell him. The apostle Paul didn't fail to do this. In his epistles he frequently expressed appreciation.

Fifthly, notice one other thing about Paul's praying. *He prayed without ceasing.* In Ephesians 1:16 Paul says, "I cease not to give thanks for you, making mention of you in my prayers." He urged the Thessalonians in 1 Thessalonians 5:17 to "pray without ceasing" and Paul set the example in this matter. He practiced what he preached.

What did Paul mean when he said that he was praying without ceasing? *Did Paul mean that he never did anything except pray?* Did he mean that he never went to sleep at night; that he prayed twenty-four hours a day? We know that is not what he meant because he did many other things. Well, what did he mean when he said that he never ceased praying for them. *One thing that he meant was that he never gave up praying. He never abandoned praying. He never said, "Well, they do not need my prayers any more. They are beyond the need of prayer."* On the other hand he never said, "They are too far gone, it is no use praying for them." He never said, "It is no use praying because I am not getting through anyway." He never said, "Well, my heart is too cold and so I might as well not pray." Paul never stopped the practice of prayer. That is what it means to pray without ceasing. It does not mean to pray every moment of the day any more than saying, "I never cease eating," means "I eat twenty-four hours a day." It means that you never abandon the practice of prayer. It means that you never give up on anybody. It means that you continue to pray for them. It means that regularly you are found in the attitude and practice of prayer.

Praying without ceasing also means that Paul was quick to go to prayer. If you grab hold of a needle on a compass, you can pull the needle away from magnetic north. But do you know what happens as soon as you let go of that needle? That needle goes right back to magnetic north. That is what ought to happen in our lives as Christians. Because of the pressure of responsibility it is sometimes impossible for us to give ourselves to prayer, but as soon as we are free again, do you know what ought to happen to us? We ought to go right back to God in prayer. That old needle of prayer ought to go right back to magnetic north. Instinctively we ought to go to God in prayer. When we are done with work and we get a moment's respite, our first thoughts ought to be, "I have to talk to my heavenly Father." This is what it means to pray without ceasing. It means that it is the instinctive reaction of our hearts to go out to God, to reach out to the Father. Whenever we are not pressed to do something else, whenever something else does not capture our attention, we ought to reach out naturally to God. In the middle of the night when we wake up, our first thoughts ought to be of God. Maybe that is why God woke us up. In the middle of the day when we are driving down the highway and see needs around us, our response ought to be to go immediately to prayer. This is part of what Paul meant when he said, "Pray without ceasing."

Romans 12:12 says, "Continuing instant in prayer." In an instant we should be in prayer. We do not need a nice quiet room. We do not need to be in the chapel. We do not need to be in a bedroom. We can be in an automobile. We can be on the football field. We can be down at the factory. But wherever we are and whenever we are, we can be in the presence of God in prayer. This is the way it was with the apostle Paul. He sometimes had a soldier chained to him when he was in prison. But that did not keep him from praying. He went to prayer instinctively. We should be like Nehemiah. Nehemiah would be working on the walls of Jerusalem and all of a sudden, in the midst of his business,

Nehemiah would be in prayer. Again and again throughout the book of Nehemiah there are these ejaculatory prayers. Very quickly, in the midst of his activities, he turns in prayer to God. The identical thing is found in Paul's epistles. He would be writing about one thing, and suddenly without warning he would shift gears and go to prayer. He did that in the book of Romans. In Romans chapters 9 through 11 he talked about election and the sovereignty of God. Then as he came to the end of this theme, suddenly Paul slipped into prayer and began to worship God. In Romans chapter 15, he exhorted the brethren, but intermixed with his exhortations are three brief prayers. Paul was quick to go to prayer. He prayed without ceasing. Is that true of us? Do our hearts instinctively run out to God? We ought to be coming to God throughout the day, saying, "Lord, help me to glorify you. Lord, teach me. Lord, show me. Lord, open doors of opportunity. Lord, deliver me from evil. Lord, watch over my eyes. Lord, take care of these ears. Lord, you know that person is going to get me upset, so please help me. Lord, give me wisdom. Lord, I am thinking of such and such a person right now. He just came to my mind. Holy Father, he has some needs. Please help him. Oh, God and Father of our Lord Jesus Christ, the Father of Glory, thank you for protecting me, preserving me, just now," etc. When someone or something comes into our minds, we ought to go to God in prayer. This is what Paul did, and we ought to follow his example.

Here, then, are some of the general characteristics of Paul's praying. I believe that the need of our time is not simply for greater theologians or greater preachers or greater talents or greater abilities or greater resources, but for men and women who know how to pray and who will pray. The Scriptures say, "the effectual fervent prayer of a righteous man availeth much" (James 5:16). We may not have great ability to preach, we may not have great resources, but Satan trembles when the weakest saint gets on his knees before God. The battles are not won when the pastor comes into the pulpit. If they are not won before he comes into the pulpit, they probably won't be won. The battles for the souls of children, or men, or women are won before the preacher ever steps into the pulpit by folks who have been on their knees before God in prayer. The ministry of the pastor from the pulpit will to a large extent be only as effective and as authoritative as the prayer lives of his congregation. Charles Spurgeon believed that the reason that he had such a powerful ministry was because he had a praying church. He said that praying people are blessed with powerful preaching. *If we want powerful preaching, we need praying people, because it is not talents or abilities alone that win or strengthen anyone. It is God who regenerates, convicts, converts, sanctifies, and empowers; and He usually moves powerfully when His people pray.* Let us therefore learn from Paul's example how to pray effectively and seek to go and do likewise.

Effectual Prayer

"The earnest, heartfelt, continued prayer of a righteous man makes tremendous power available, dynamic in the working" (James 5:16b, Amplified Version).

Scriptural Patterns for Prayer

A. Matthew 6:9-13

1. *"Our Father":* These words remind us of the love and nearness of God. We should *worship and praise God* for His marvelous works in saving us, enabling us to have the power to become sons of God.

2. *"Which art in heaven":* Who is our God? He is a God of majesty who demands our respect and reverence. We ought to worship Him for His sovereign control over the earth.

3. *"Hallowed be thy name":* The first of these requests has to do with God's concerns. We ought to pray that we will be brought to reverence and glorify His name, as His name represents aspects of His character. Pray for increased holiness of life. Pray for the lost that through their salvation God's name will be glorified.

4. *"Thy kingdom come":* Give praise to God that the King *has come* and provided salvation for His own. Pray for unsaved loved ones and neighbors. Pray that by the power of the Holy Spirit people around the world will experience conversion and thereby acknowledge Jesus Christ as King of their lives. Pray also that the King will come. The last prayer of the Bible is "Even so come, Lord Jesus."

5. *"Thy will be done on earth as it is in heaven":* Pray that we will do God's will as the angels do it—exclusively, universally (to any extent), immediately, continually, and delightfully. Pray daily for help to will and to do of His good pleasure (Philippians 2:13).

6. *"Give us this day our daily bread":* Pray that God will meet our physical needs, that we may have strength to honor His name, spread His kingdom, and do His will. These are our reasons for living. Pray that we will daily and consciously depend on Him for our physical needs. Be thankful to God for all physical provisions. He is the source of all we have.

7. *"And forgive us our debts, as we forgive our debtors":* These next two petitions have to do with confession and maintaining a right relationship with God. We ought to know mourning over our sin, which dishonors His name, His kingdom, and keeps us from doing His will. If we experience forgiveness for our mountains of iniquity, we will be forgiving others.

8. *"Deliver us from evil":* Our greatest longing is to please our Father. Pray that we will not be brought into that place where we are overcome by temptation. Pray that if we do experience temptation we will be delivered from the evil one and the evil world. Why do we want to be holy? That we may honor His name, spread His kingdom, and do His will. Most of our praying for ourselves should be over our concern to be holy men. Too often we put our wants first instead of God's concerns. Much blessing will be ours when we obey Jesus' command to pray after this pattern.

B. In James 5:16-19 we see a pattern for prayer in Elijah.

1. *He prayed pointedly.* He prayed for specific requests—no rain for three years and six months.

2. *He prayed passionately.* He prayed earnestly.

3. *He prayed perseveringly.* He prayed and it didn't rain; then he prayed again and again until he received the answer.

How to Pray

Session No. 1

A. Consider the following Old Testament examples of prayer. Pay attention to the circumstances in which they prayed, how, when, where, and what they prayed, whether the prayer was answered specifically, the elements of the prayer, the vocabulary they used, the length of the prayer, and how it is similar and different from other examples you study.

1. Abraham, Genesis 18:22-33

    a. Intercessory prayer—for others—v. 25.
    b. Specific—v. 24.
    c. Pleaded attributes of God—v. 25.
    d. Humble, reverent, and yet bold—vv. 27, 32.
    e. Persistent—v. 27.
    f. While standing before God—v. 22.
    g. For the safety of the righteous—v. 23.
    h. Antiphonal—Abraham speaks, then God speaks.
    i. Requests became bigger.
    j. Was answered.

2. Isaac, Genesis 25:19-21

    a. ______________________________

    b. ______________________________

    c. ______________________________

    d. ______________________________

e. ________________________________

f. ________________________________

g. ________________________________

3. Moses, Exodus 32:31-33

a. ________________________________

b. ________________________________

c. ________________________________

d. ________________________________

e. ________________________________

f. ________________________________

4. Manoah, Judges 13:6-9

a. ________________________________

b. ________________________________

c. ________________________________

d. ________________________________

e. ________________________________

f. ________________________________

5. Hannah, 1 Samuel 1:1-11

   a. ______________________________

   b. ______________________________

   c. ______________________________

   d. ______________________________

   e. ______________________________

   f. ______________________________

6. Samuel, 1 Samuel 7:5-9

   a. ______________________________

   b. ______________________________

   c. ______________________________

   d. ______________________________

   e. ______________________________

   f. ______________________________

   g. ______________________________

7. Elijah, 1 Kings 18:36-39

   a. ______________________________

   b. ______________________________

c. ______________________________

d. ______________________________

e. ______________________________

f. ______________________________

g. ______________________________

8. Elisha, 2 Kings 4:22-33

a. ______________________________

b. ______________________________

c. ______________________________

d. ______________________________

e. ______________________________

f. ______________________________

g. ______________________________

h. ______________________________

i. ______________________________

9. Hezekiah, 2 Kings 20:1-6

a. ______________________________

b. ______________________________

c. ____________________

d. ____________________

e. ____________________

f. ____________________

g. ____________________

10. Job, Job 42:1-6

a. ____________________

b. ____________________

c. ____________________

d. ____________________

e. ____________________

f. ____________________

g. ____________________

11. Daniel, Daniel 6:4-11

a. ____________________

b. ____________________

c. ____________________

d. ____________________

e. ______________________________

f. ______________________________

g. ______________________________

h. ______________________________

12. Jonah, Jonah 2:1-2

a. ______________________________

b. ______________________________

c. ______________________________

d. ______________________________

e. ______________________________

f. ______________________________

g. ______________________________

h. ______________________________

B. List the personal insights, challenges, and impact you have received for your prayer life from this study. Be specific and personal.

1. ______________________________

2. ______________________________

3. ______________________________

4. ____

5. ____

6. ____

7. ____

8. ____

9. ____

10. ____

How to Pray

Session No. 2

A. Consider the following New Testament examples of prayer. Note every detail you can.

1. Jesus, Mark 1:32-39

   a. After a very busy day.

   b. After a very successful day.

   c. Before a new venture.

   d. ______________________________

   e. ______________________________

   f. ______________________________

   g. ______________________________

   h. ______________________________

   i. ______________________________

   j. ______________________________

2. Bartimaeus, Mark 10:46-52

   a. ______________________________

   b. ______________________________

   c. ______________________________

d. ______________________________

e. ______________________________

f. ______________________________

g. ______________________________

h. ______________________________

i. ______________________________

3. Anna, Luke 2:37, 38

a. ______________________________

b. ______________________________

c. ______________________________

d. ______________________________

e. ______________________________

f. ______________________________

g. ______________________________

h. ______________________________

4. Publican, Luke 18:9-14

a. ______________________________

b. ______________________________

c. ______________________________

d. ______________________________

e. ______________________________

f. ______________________________

g. ______________________________

5. Early church, Acts, 4:24-31

a. ______________________________

b. ______________________________

c. ______________________________

d. ______________________________

e. ______________________________

f. ______________________________

g. ______________________________

6. Stephen, Acts 7:54-60

a. ______________________________

b. ______________________________

c. ______________________________

d. ______________________________

e. ______________________________

f. ______________________________

g. ______________________________

7. Peter, Acts 9:36-43

a. ______________________________

b. ______________________________

c. ______________________________

d. ______________________________

e. ______________________________

f. ______________________________

g. ______________________________

8. Cornelius, Acts 10:1-6, 30

a. ______________________________

b. ______________________________

c. ______________________________

d. ______________________________

e. ______________________________

f. ______________________________

g. ______________________________

9. Paul and Silas, Acts 16:16-25

   a. ____________________

   b. ____________________

   c. ____________________

   d. ____________________

   e. ____________________

   f. ____________________

   g. ____________________

10. Paul, Acts 28:1-8

   a. ____________________

   b. ____________________

   c. ____________________

   d. ____________________

   e. ____________________

   f. ____________________

   g. ____________________

11. Early church, Acts 1:12-26

   a. ____________________

b. ______________________________

c. ______________________________

d. ______________________________

e. ______________________________

f. ______________________________

g. ______________________________

h. ______________________________

12. Early church, Acts 12:1-11

a. ______________________________

b. ______________________________

c. ______________________________

d. ______________________________

e. ______________________________

f. ______________________________

g. ______________________________

B. List the personal insights, challenges, and impact you received for your prayer life from this study. Be specific and personal.

1. ______________________________

2. ______________________________

3. ______________________________

4. ______________________________

5. ______________________________

6. ______________________________

7. ______________________________

8. ______________________________

9. ______________________________

10. ______________________________

How to Pray

Session No. 3

A. Think about the importance of prayer in the life of the individual Christian, in the church, and in Christian service.

1. How do we know prayer is important for the individual Christian, for the church, for Christian service?

____

____

____

2. Why is prayer so important? List all of the reasons you can think of as to why we should pray.

a. ____

b. ____

c. ____

d. ____

e. ____

f. ____

B. Think about the biblical principles of acceptable prayer suggested by these verses. Answer the question – how are God the Father, God the Son, God the Holy Spirit involved in our prayers?

1. Matthew 6:9; Ephesians 3:14 ____________________

____

____

2. Hebrews 4:14-16; 1 Timothy 2:5; Hebrews 10:19-22; John 14:14; 16:24

____

____

3. Romans 8:26; Jude 20; Ephesians 6:18 __________

____

____

4. 1 John 5:14,15 ______________________________

____

____

5. Hebrews 11:6; James 1:5-8 ____________________

____

____

6. James 5:16 ______________________________

____

____

7. 1 John 3:21, 22 ___________________________

____

____

8. Matthew 26:39 ___________________________

____

____

9. John 15:7-11 ____________________________

____

____

10. Psalm 10:17; 138:6; Isaiah 66:2 _____________

____

____

C. Consider the hindrances to effective prayer. What hindrances are suggested by—

1. Psalm 66:18; Proverbs 28:9; Isaiah 59:2-8 ______

____

____

2. James 4:1-6 __________________________________

____

____

3. Matthew 21:22 ______________________________

____

____

4. Matthew 6:7-8 ______________________________

____

____

5. James 1:5-7; Matthew 13:58 ________________

____

____

6. Luke 6:38; Proverbs 21:13; 28:27 ____________

____

____

7. Luke 18:11 __________________________________

____

____

8. Ezekiel 14:3-8 ______________________________

____

____

9. Mark 11:12-25 ______________________________

____

____

10. Matthew 5:22-24 ___________________________

____

____

11. 1 Peter 3:7 _______________________________

____

____

D. Identify the hindrances in your life.

1. ____

2. ____

3. ____

4. ____

5. ____

6. ____

7. ____

E. List the personal insights or challenges you have received through this study for your own prayer life. How should your prayer life be different?

1. ____

2. ____

3. ____

4. ____

5. ____

6. ____

7. ____

8. ____

9. ____

How to Pray

Session No. 4

A. Consider the matter of the best time and place to pray.

1. Should we set aside a specific time and place for prayer? If not why not? Consider Luke 5:16; Daniel 10:1-3; 6:10; Acts 3:1; 10:3, 30; Psalm 55:16, 17; 5:3; 141:2; Genesis 19:27; Job 1:5.

____

____

____

2. When and where is the best time and place for you to have your specific times of prayer? Why? Consider the previous Scripture verses.

____

____

____

3. Why is the morning a good time for extended prayer? Why is the evening a good time for extended prayer?

____

____

____

4. How should morning prayer differ from evening prayer?

____

____

____

B. Consider the length of prayers.

1. Do prayers have to be long to be effective? 1 Kings 17:20-21; Matthew 6:7.

____

____

____

2. Are there times when long prayers are called for? Daniel 10:2, 3,12; Luke 6:12, 13; Acts 12:5; 1 Kings 8:22-53.

____

____

____

3. How long should our prayers be?

____

____

____

C. Consider the vocabulary of prayer.

1. How would you characterize the words used in the following prayers?

   a. Acts 4:24-30 ______________________________

   ____

   b. John 17:1-26 ______________________________

   ____

   c. Matthew 6:9-13 ____________________________

   ____

   d. Matthew 15:22-28 __________________________

   ____

   e. 1 Kings 18:36, 37 __________________________

   ____

2. How would you characterize the words used in your prayers? Do you use clichés or stereotyped phrases, or outdated words, or words which have no meaning to you or to others? Do you pray with understanding? Make a list of all phrases and words which you have heard used in prayers that you think ought to be avoided, changed, or used less. What problems in the vocabulary of prayer should we avoid?

   a. ____

b. ______________________________

c. ______________________________

d. ______________________________

e. ______________________________

3. List the personal insights or challenges you have received through this study for your own prayer life.

a. ______________________________

b. ______________________________

c. ______________________________

d. ______________________________

e. ______________________________

f. ______________________________

g. ______________________________

h. ______________________________

How to Pray

Session No. 5

A. Consider the different elements that may be included in prayer.

1. Identify the elements in the following verses.

a. John 4:23; Revelation 4:11

____

b. Psalm 107:8; Hebrews 13:15

____

c. Study Psalm 103 and note at least 15 things for which the Psalmist praised God.

1. ______________________________

2. ______________________________

3. ______________________________

4. ______________________________

5. ______________________________

6. ______________________________

7. ______________________________

8. ______________________________

9. ______________________________

10. ______________________________

11. ______________________________

12. ______________________________

13. ______________________________

14. ______________________________

15. ______________________________

d. Philippians 4:6

____

e. Psalm 51; Ezra 9:5-15

____

f. 1 Timothy 2:1

____

g. 1 Peter 2:5; Romans 12:1

____

2. Is it necessary for all elements to be in every prayer?

____

3. What might cause you to vary the elements?

____

____

4. How do adoration, praise, and thanksgiving differ?

____

____

B. Consider the pattern prayer of Jesus in Matthew 6:9-13.

1. Why is it important to begin our prayers as Jesus taught us?

____

____

2. Summarize the basic petitions of this prayer. (Compare the brief exposition of this prayer included in the introductory reading.)

a. ______________________________________

b. ______________________________________

c. ______________________________________

d. ______________________________________

e. ______________________________________

f. ______________________________________

g. ______________________________________

3. List the requests that are primarily related to God.

____

4. List the requests that are primarily related to man's needs.

____

5. List the requests centered around spiritual needs and those emphasizing physical needs.

Spiritual ________________________________

Physical ________________________________

6. What lessons may we learn about prayer from this passage?

a. ____________________________________

b. ____________________________________

c. ____________________________________

d. ____________________________________

e. ____________________________________

f. ____________________________________

C. Consider Christ's prayer in John 17.

1. For whom did He pray?

a. Verses 1, 5 ____________________________

b. Verse 9 ____________________

c. Verse 20 ____________________

2. For what did He pray?

a. Verses 1,5 ____________________

b. Verse 11 ____________________

c. Verse 13 ____________________

d. Verse 15 ____________________

e. Verse 17 ____________________

f. Verse 19 ____________________

g. Verse 21 ____________________

h. Verse 23 ____________________

i. Verse 24 ____________________

j. Verse 26 ____________________

3. In what specific ways can this prayer help you in praying?

a. ____________________

b. ____________________

c. ____________________

d. ____________________

How to Pray

Session No. 6

A. What prayer requests are suggested by the following verses? These are things God wants us to pray for (1 John 5:14, 15).

1. Romans 10:1 ______________________________

2. Ephesians 1:16-18 ___________________________

3. Ephesians 3:14-16 ___________________________

4. Ephesians 3:17 ____________________________

5. Ephesians 3:18 ____________________________

6. Ephesians 3:19 ____________________________

7. Philippians 1:9-11 ___________________________

8. Colossians 1:9, 10 ___________________________

9. 1 Thessalonians 3:11, 12 ______________________

10. 2 Thessalonians 2:16, 17 ______________________

11. 1 Timothy 2:1-3 ____________________________

12. Matthew 9:36-38 ____________________________

13. Psalm 19:13, 14 ____________________________

14. Psalm 37:5 ________________________________

15. Psalm 51:10-12 ______________________________

16. Psalm 119:34 ______________________________

17. Psalm 119:133 ______________________________

18. Psalm 119:117 ______________________________

19. Psalm 141:3 ______________________________

20. Psalm 86:11; 25:4 ______________________________

21. Psalm 119:18 ______________________________

22. James 1:5 ______________________________

23. James 5:16 ______________________________

24. Colossians 4:3; 2 Thessalonians 3:1 ______________

____

25. Ephesians 6:18 ______________________________

26. Psalm 122:6 ______________________________

27. Matthew 5:44 ______________________________

B. Are there petitions found in the aforementioned verses for which you do not pray? List them and include them in your prayers.

1. ______________________________

2. ______________________________

3. ______________________________

4. ______________________________

5. ______________________________

6. ______________________________

7. ______________________________

8. ______________________________

9. ______________________________

10. ______________________________

C. Consider the importance of praying in a group.

1. Look up the following verses and note what they teach about the practice of group praying.

a. Matthew 18:19, 20 ____________________

____

b. Galatians 6:2 ____________________

____

c. Acts 21:1-5 ____________________

____

d. Acts 1:12-14 ____________________

____

e. Acts 2:42 ______________________

____

f. Acts 3:1 ______________________

____

g. Acts 4:24-31 ______________________

____

h. Acts 8:15 ______________________

____

i. Acts 12:5, 13 ______________________

____

j. Acts 13:1-3 ______________________

____

2. What are the benefits of group prayer?

a. ______________________

b. ______________________

c. ______________________

d. ______________________

3. List as many reasons as you can why Christians do not pray together more.

a. ____

b. ____

c. ____

d. ____

e. ____

f. ____

g. ____

h. ____

4. Make a list of principles or suggested procedures for group prayer. How can our group praying be improved?

a. ____

b. ____

c. ____

d. ____

e. ____

f. ____

g. ____

h. ____

i. ______________________________

j. ______________________________

k. ______________________________

D. List any personal challenges or insights you received from this study for your prayer life.

1. ______________________________

2. ______________________________

3. ______________________________

4. ______________________________

5. ______________________________

6. ______________________________

How to Pray

Session No. 7

A. Identify the problems you face in your prayer life.

1. ____________________________________

2. ____________________________________

3. ____________________________________

4. ____________________________________

5. ____________________________________

6. ____________________________________

7. ____________________________________

8. ____________________________________

9. ____________________________________

10. ____________________________________

B. Consider the following problems and suggest solutions.

1. The problem of mind wandering when you pray or when others are praying. What causes these problems? What should you do when this happens?

____

____

____

2. The problem of not being in the mood for prayer. Should you pray only when you are in the mood? Is it hypocrisy to pray when you don't feel like it?

____

____

____

3. The problem of neglect. Why do we neglect prayer? How can we solve this problem?

____

____

____

4. The problem of monotonous repetition. What are its causes? How can it be solved?

____

____

____

5. The problem of praying in public. What are its causes? How can it be solved?

____

____

____

6. Other problems you would like to discuss.

____

____

____

C. List any ways in which this study on "How to Pray" has benefited you.

1. ____
2. ____
3. ____
4. ____
5. ____
6. ____
7. ____
8. ____
9. ____
10. ____
11. ____

Suggested Pointers on Prayer

A. How to Set Up a Prayer List

A prayer list is to be an aid to your memory. For it to be useful, you should not feel bound to it, but, being in the spirit of prayer, never let it be a cold form. Keep revising it.

1. Have one sheet for temporary prayer requests. This may change every week. Pray about special problems and opportunities facing you the coming week or month.

2. Have a sheet for daily requests. These are requests of a more permanent nature that you want to remember daily such as: your family (pinpoint what you want God to do in them), your own spiritual needs; your unsaved friends; your Christian friends, your prayer partner's needs; your Christian service opportunities; your church and its leaders and members.

3. Have a sheet for once-a-week prayer requests. Missions can be divided up so you pray for a different area of the world each day, thus going around the world each week in prayer: Monday in Latin America; Tuesday in Africa; Wednesday, Europe; Thursday, Northeast Asia; Friday, Southwest Asia; Saturday, the Islands; and Sunday, North America.

   You can add prayer helps to your list by having a sheet for prayer promises, special prayers, and hymns to aid you in prayer.

B. How to Pray for Missionaries

Find out all you can about the missionaries for whom you are praying by regular correspondence and then pray regularly, intelligently, and perseveringly for specific needs. Here are some suggestions from missionaries regarding their needs.

1. Pray that we will be enabled to establish local churches where God's people will be articulate in the truth and be full of spiritual discernment.

2. Pray that God will keep us from being too busy—even serving God—to pray.

3. Pray that God will strengthen us to resist temptation, loneliness, discouragement, and impatience.

4. Pray that God will keep alive the fires of compassion for the lost.

5. Pray not only that God will bless our activities but that He will censor them, too.

6. Pray that God will give us an unconquerable determination to go all the way with Him, rather than that He will remove obstacles.

7. Pray for essentials, that God will give us the measure of health that will best glorify Him.

C. How to Pray for All Saints (Ephesians 6:18).

Let us claim by faith the following petitions for each other (Mark 11:22-26; Matthew 17:20; Matthew 18:19, 20). Pray:

1. That all of us might be soundly converted to Christ (Acts 2:39; 1 Timothy 2:1-6; Romans 10:1).

2. That Christ may be seen in our every action in the home, in the school, down at the job, etc. (Ephesians 5:18; Ephesians 6:9; Matthew 5:13-16).

3. That we would each fulfill our part and use our gifts to build up the body of Christ which is His church (Romans 12; Ephesians 4:12-16).

4. That each of us would have increasing boldness and power to witness (Ephesians 6:19; Acts 4:20, 31).

5. That we might have open doors (opportunities) to witness (Colossians 4:3; Colossians 3:17; 1 Corinthians 16:9).

6. That each of us may have an increasing understanding of, and the power to obey the will of God (Colossians 1:9-11; Colossians 2:2).

7. That each of us may constantly and increasingly manifest the fruit of the Spirit (Galatians 5:22, 23; Philippians 1:9-11).

8. That we may be able to rejoice and be content in whatever circumstances we find ourselves (Philippians 4:4-13).

9. That God might heal us when we are sick, if it be His will (James 5:13-16; Psalm 103:3, 4; 2 Corinthians 12:7-10).

10. For specific requests and needs to be supplied for our good and God's glory (John 14:13-15; Philippians 4:19; Philippians 4:6).

"Pray for one another"—James 5:16.
"Pray without ceasing"—1 Thessalonians 5:17.
"Brethren, pray for us"—1 Thessalonians 5:25.

Remember, at the judgment seat of Christ it will be too late to discover that prayer is a must.

Prayer Sheet No. 1

Temporary Requests

	Requests	*Date Began Praying*	*Date Answered*
1.			
2.			
3.			
4.			
5.			
6.			
7.			
8.			
9.			
10.			
11.			
12.			
13.			
14.			

15. ______________________________

16. ______________________________

17. ______________________________

18. ______________________________

19. ______________________________

20. ______________________________

21. ______________________________

22. ______________________________

23. ______________________________

24. ______________________________

25. ______________________________

26. ______________________________

27. ______________________________

28 ______________________________

29. ______________________________

30. ______________________________

Prayer Sheet No. 2

More Than
Once-a-Week Prayer Requests

1. ______________________________

2. ______________________________

3. ______________________________

4. ______________________________

5. ______________________________

6. ______________________________

7. ______________________________

8. ______________________________

9. ______________________________

10. ______________________________

11. ______________________________

12. ______________________________

13. ______________________________

14. ______________________________

15. ______________________________

16. ______________________________

17. ______________________________

18. ______________________________

19. ______________________________

20. ______________________________

21. ______________________________

22. ______________________________

23. ______________________________

24. ______________________________

25. ______________________________

26. ______________________________

27. ______________________________

28 ______________________________

29. ______________________________

30. ______________________________

Prayer Sheet No. 3

Once-a-Week Prayer Requests

A. Sunday

1. ____________________
2. ____________________
3. ____________________
4. ____________________
5. ____________________
6. ____________________
7. ____________________
8. ____________________
9. ____________________
10. ____________________

B. Monday

1. ____________________
2. ____________________
3. ____________________
4. ____________________

5. ______________________________

6. ______________________________

7. ______________________________

8. ______________________________

9. ______________________________

10. ______________________________

C. Tuesday

1. ______________________________

2. ______________________________

3. ______________________________

4. ______________________________

5. ______________________________

6. ______________________________

7. ______________________________

8. ______________________________

9. ______________________________

10. ______________________________

D. Wednesday

1. ______________________________
2. ______________________________
3. ______________________________
4. ______________________________
5. ______________________________
6. ______________________________
7. ______________________________
8. ______________________________
9. ______________________________
10. ______________________________

E. Thursday

1. ______________________________
2. ______________________________
3. ______________________________
4. ______________________________
5. ______________________________
6. ______________________________
7. ______________________________

8. ______________________________

9. ______________________________

10. ______________________________

F. Friday

1. ______________________________

2. ______________________________

3. ______________________________

4. ______________________________

5. ______________________________

6. ______________________________

7. ______________________________

8. ______________________________

9. ______________________________

10. ______________________________

G. Saturday

1. ______________________________

2. ______________________________

3. ______________________________

4. ____

5. ____

6. ____

7. ____

8. ____

9. ____

10. ____

ENDNOTES

---

[1] A. T. Pierson, *George Mueller All Things Are Possible* (Greenville, S.C.: Emerald Int. Pub., 1999), 10.
[2] George Mueller and A. E. C. Brooks, *Answers to Prayer* (Chicago: Moody Press, 1984), 47.
[3] Ibid., 48.
[4] Ibid., 54.
[5] Ibid., 55.
[6] Ibid., 9.
[7] Ibid., 31.
[8] Ibid., 14-15.
[9] Ibid., 19.
[10] A. T. Pierson, *George Mueller of Bristol*, (Pasadena: Wipf and Stock 1999), 158.
[11] Roger Steer, *George Mueller Delighted in God* (Colorado Springs: Harold Shaw Publishers, 1997), 183.
[12] George Mueller, *Answers to Prayer*, 32.
[13] Ibid., 117.
[14] Roger Steer, *George Mueller Delighted in God*, 109.
[15] George Mueller, *Answers to Prayer*, 33-34.
[16] Roger Steer, *George Mueller Delighted in God*, 130.
[17] A. T. Pierson, *George Mueller of Bristol*, 458.
[18] Roger Steer, *George Mueller Delighted in God*, 311.
[19] George Mueller, *Answers to Prayer*, 116.
[20] Roger Steer, *George Mueller Delighted in God*, 317.
[21] Ibid., 337.
[22] Ibid., 319.
[23] Ibid., 266-267.
[24] George Mueller, *Answers to Prayer*, 73.
[25] Ibid., 50.
[26] Roger Steer, *George Mueller Delighted in God*, 310.
[27] George Mueller, *Answers to Prayer,* 46.
[28] Basil Miller, *George Mueller, Man of Faith and Miracles* (Minneapolis: Bethany House, 1972), 57.
[29] George Mueller, *Answers to Prayer*, 25-26.
[30] Roger Steer, *George Mueller Delighted in God*, 331.
[31] George Mueller, *Answers to Prayer*, 15).
[32] A. T. Pierson, *George Mueller of Bristol*, 456.
[33] Roger Steer, *George Mueller Delighted in God*, 257.
[34] Jack Hughes, *Expository Preaching with Word Pictures* (Rosshire, Great Britain: Christian Focus Pub., 2001), 248-249.

[35] Charles H. Spurgeon, *True Prayer-True Power!* (1860). Retrieved Feb. 27, 2003, from http://www.spurgeon.org/sermons/0328.htm.
[36] John Piper, *The Pleasures of God* (Portland, Ore.: Multnomah, 1991), 232.
[37] Austin Phelps, *The Still Hour* (Carlisle, Pa.: The Banner of Truth, 1974), 28.
[38] Roger Nicole, "Prayer: The Prelude to Revival," *Reformation and Revival Journal* 1, no. 3 (Summer 1992): 26.
[39] Ibid., 27, (author's paraphrased).
[40] Charles H. Spurgeon, *Let Us Pray* (1859). Retrieved Feb. 27, 2003, from http://www.biblebb.com/files/spurgeon/0288.htm.
[41] Austin Phelps, *The Still Hour*, 31.

Disciplined Bible Study

Introduction

This unit is designed as a "study manual" to help the student learn how to develop a disciplined habit of reading the Bible with great profit. It begins with some outstanding introductory readings by Thomas Watson, J. C. Ryle and C. H. Spurgeon. I have included these studies rather than writing something new because these authors have already said, so very well, the very points I think must be made. These introductory readings are followed by thought-provoking questions and case studies, which we hope will lead the student into a comprehensive and practical study designed to equip you to get the most out of your Bible study.

Many of the questions asked and case studies presented will be answered by the introductory readings. However, this unit of the manual is intended to stimulate you to do some hard thinking on your own. Therefore, to answer some of the questions, you will be directed to the Scripture passages, which will require you to search and think for yourself.

At the end of this unit a list of helpful books and tapes on Bible study is included.

To gain the most from these studies, we recommend that you read the introductory materials first and then proceed to the questions and case studies. The questions are divided into seven sessions. Each session may be studied, one at a time; or, if desired, each session may be broken down into small segments.

Profiting From the Word of God

By Thomas Watson
(c. 1620-1686)

This is the final article in a two-part classic study on the right way to approach the reading of the Bible, God's Holy Word. The author is Thomas Watson, a seventeenth century pastor and teacher. The main bulk of this study consists of directions on how to approach reading the Bible. In the first part, the following directions were given:

I. Remove those things which will hinder your profiting from reading scripture.
II. Prepare your hearts for the reading of the Word.
III. Read the scripture with reverence.
IV. Read the books of scripture in order.
V. Get a right understanding of scripture.
VI. Read the word with seriousness.
VII. Labor to remember what you read.
VIII. Meditate upon what you read.
IX. Come to the reading of scripture with humble hearts.
X. Give credence to the word written.
XI. Highly prize the scriptures.
XII. Get an ardent love for the Word.

Now here, we continue this study. May the Lord bless you as you read and apply this study.

How We May Read the Scriptures with Most Spiritual Profit

"And it shall be with him, and he shall read therein all the days of his life: that he may learn

to fear the LORD his God, to keep all the words of this law and these statutes, to do them" (Deuteronomy 17:19). [Footnote #8]

DIRECTION XIII. *Come to the reading of the word with honest hearts.*--Christ speaks of "the honest heart" (Luke 8:15).

QUESTION. "What is it to read the word with an honest heart?"

ANSWER 1. *To come with an heart willing to know the whole counsel of God.*--A good heart would not have any truth concealed; but saith, as Job, "That which I see not, teach thou me" (Job 34:32). When men pick and choose in religion, they will do some things the word enjoins them, but not others. These are unsound hearts, and are not benefited by holy writ. These are like a patient, who having a bitter pill prescribed, and a julep, he will take the julep, but refuseth the pill.

2. To read the word with an honest heart, is *to read it that we may be made better by it.*--The word is the medium and organ of sanctity; and we come to it not only to illuminate us, but consecrate us: "Sanctify them through thy truth" (John 17:17). Some go to the Bible, as one goes to the garden, to pick flowers, that is, fine notions. Austin confesseth, that before his conversion he went to hear Ambrose more for the elegancy of speech and quaintness of notion, than the spirituality of the matter. This is like a woman that paints her face, but neglects her health. But *this* is to have an honest heart, when we come to the scriptures as Naaman to the waters of Jordan, to be healed of our leprosy. "O," saith the soul, "that this sword of the Spirit may pierce the rock of my heart; that this blessed word may have such a virtue in it, as the water of jealousy, to kill and make fruitful (See Numbers

5:27-28); that it may kill my sin, and make me fruitful in grace."

DIRECTION XIV. *Learn to apply scripture.*--Take every word as spoken to yourselves. When the word thunders against sin, think thus: "God means my sins"; when it presseth any duty, "God intends me in this." Many put off scripture from themselves, as if it only concerned those who lived in the time when it was written; but if you intend to profit by the word, bring it home to yourselves: a medicine will do no good, unless it be applied. The saints of old took the word as if it had been spoken to them by name. When King Josiah heard the threatening which was written in the book of God, he applied it to himself: "He rent his clothes, and humbled" his soul "before the Lord" (2 Kings 22:11,13).

DIRECTION XV. *Observe the preceptive part of the word, as well as the promissive.*--The precepts carry duty in them, like the veins which carry the blood; the promises carry comfort in them, like the arteries which carry the spirits. Make use as well of the precepts to direct you, as the promises to comfort you. Such as cast their eye upon the promise, with a neglect of the command, are not edified by scripture; they look more after comfort than duty. They mistake their comforts, as Apollo embraced the laurel-tree instead of Daphne. The body may be swelled with wind as well as flesh: a man may be filled with false comfort, as well as that which is genuine and real.

DIRECTION XVI. *Let your thoughts dwell upon the most material passages of scripture.*--The bee fastens on those flowers where she may suck most sweetness. Though the whole contexture of scripture is excellent, yet some parts of it may have a greater emphasis, and be more quick and pungent. Reading the names of the tribes, or the genealogies of the patriarchs, is not of the same importance as faith and "the new creature" (2 Corinthians 5:17). Mind the *magnalia legis*, the "weighty things of the law" (Hosea 8:12). They who read only to satisfy their curiosity, do rather busy than profit themselves. The searching too far into Christ's temporal reign hath, I fear, weakened his spiritual reign in some men's hearts.

DIRECTION XVII. *Compare yourselves with the word.*--See how the scripture and your hearts agree, how your dial goes with this sun. Are your hearts, as it were, a transcript and counterpane of scripture? Is the word copied out into your hearts? The word calls for humility; are you not only humbled, but humble? The word calls for regeneration (John 3:7); have you the signature and engraving of the Holy Ghost upon you? Have you a change of heart? Not only a partial moral change, but a spiritual? Is there such a change wrought in you, as if another soul did live in the same body? "Such were some of you; but ye are washed, but ye are sanctified," etc. (1 Corinthians 6:11). The word calls for love to the saints (1 Peter 1:22); do you love grace where you see it? Do you love grace in a poor man as well as in a rich? A son loves to see his father's picture, though hung in a mean frame; do you love grace, though mixed with some failings, as we love gold, though it be in the ore? The bringing the rule of the word and our hearts together, to see how they agree, would prove very advantageous to us. Hereby we come to know the true complexion and state of our souls, and see what evidences and certificates we have for heaven.

DIRECTION XVIII. *Take special notice of those scriptures which speak to your particular case.*--Were a consumptive person to read Galen or Hippocrates, he would chiefly observe what they writ about a consumption. Great regard is to be had to those paragraphs of scripture, which are most apposite to one's present case. I shall instance only in three cases: 1. Affliction. 2. Desertion. 3. Sin.

CASE I. First, *Affliction.--Hath God made your chain heavy?* Consult these scriptures: "If ye endure chastening, God dealeth with you as sons" (Hebrews 12:7; See also Job 36:8-9; Deuteronomy 8:15; 1 Kings 11:39; Psalm 89:30-33; Hebrews 12:10-11; Psalm 37:39; Romans 8:28; 1 Peter 1:6-7; 2 Chronicles 33:11-13; Revelation 3:19; 2 Corinthians 4:16; Job 5:17; Micah 6:9). "By this shall the iniquity of Jacob be purged; and this is all the fruit to take away his sin" (Isaiah 27:9). "Your sorrow shall be turned into joy" (John 16:20). The French have a berry, which they call *uve de spine*, "the grape of a thorn". God gives joy out of sorrow; here is the grape of a thorn: "Our light affliction, which is but for a moment, worketh for us a far more exceeding and eternal weight of glory" (2 Corinthians 4:17). The limner lays his gold upon dark colours: God first lays the dark colour of affliction, and then the golden colour of glory.

CASE II. Secondly, *Desertion.--Are your spiritual comforts eclipsed?* "In a little wrath I hid my face from thee for a moment: but with everlasting kindness will I have mercy on thee" (Isaiah 54:8. See also Lamentations 3:31-33; Psalm 106:6,9; 103:9; Mark 15:34; Isaiah 8:17; 49:15; 50:10; 54:10; 2 Corinthians 7:6). The sun may hide itself in a cloud, but it is not out of the firmament; God may hide his face, but he is not out of covenant. "I will not be always wroth: for the spirit should fail before me, and the souls which I have made" (Isaiah 57:16). God is like the musician, He will not stretch the strings of His lute too hard lest they break. "Light is sown for the righteous" (Psalm 97:11). A saint's comfort may be hid as seed under the clods, but at last it will spring up into an harvest of joy.

CASE III. Thirdly, *Sin.*--1. *Are you drawn away with lust?* Read Galations 5:24; James 1:15; 1 Peter 2:11: "Abstain from fleshly lusts, which war against the soul." Lust kills the embracing. "There met him a woman with the attire of an harlot. He goeth after her straightway, as an ox goeth to the slaughter; till a dart strike through his liver," etc. (Proverbs 7:10,22,23). "The mouth of strange women is a deep pit: he that is abhorred of the Lord shall fall therein" (Proverbs 22:14). Go to the waters of the sanctuary to quench the fire of lust.

2. *Are you under the power of unbelief?*--Read Isaiah 26:3: "Thou wilt keep him in perfect peace, whose mind is stayed on thee: because he trusteth in Thee." Mr. Bolton speaks of a distressed soul who found much comfort from this scripture on his sick bed: "The word of the Lord is tried: He is a buckler to all them that trust in Him" (2 Samuel 22:31. See also Zephaniah 3:12; Ps. 34:22; 55:22; 32:10; Mark 9:23; 1 Peter 5:7). "That whosoever believeth in Him should not perish" (John 3:15). Unbelief is a God-affronting sin: "He that believeth not God, hath made him a liar" (1 John 5:10). It is a soul-murdering sin: "He that believeth not the Son shall not see life; but the wrath of God abideth on him" (John 3:36). Thus, in reading observe those scriptures which do *rem acu tangere*, "touch upon your particular case". Although all the Bible must be read; yet those texts which point most directly to your condition, be sure to put a special star upon.

DIRECTION XIX. *Take special notice of the examples in scripture.*--Make the examples of others living sermons to you.

1. *Observe the examples of God's judgments upon sinners.*--They have been hanged up in chains *in terrorem.* How severely hath God punished proud men! Nebuchadnezzar was turned to grass, Herod eaten up with vermin. How hath God plagued idolaters! (See Numbers 25:3-5,9; 1 Kings 14:9-11). What a swift witness hath He been against liars! (See Acts 5:5,10). These examples are set-up as sea-marks to avoid. (See 1 Corinthians 10:11; Jude 7).

2. *Observe the examples of God's mercy to saints.*--Jeremiah was preserved in the dungeon, the three children in the furnace, Daniel in the lion's den. These examples are props to faith, spurs to holiness.

DIRECTION XX. *Leave not off reading in the Bible till you find your hearts warmed.*-- "I will never forget thy precepts: for with them thou hast quickened me" (Psalm 119:93). Read the word, not only as a history, but labour to be affected with it. Let it not only inform you, but inflame you. "`Is not my word like as a fire?' saith the Lord" (Jeremiah 23:29). Go not from the word till you can say as those disciples, "Did not our heart burn within us?" (Luke 24:32).

DIRECTION XXI. *Set upon the practice of what you read.*-- "I have done Thy commandments" (Psalm 119:166). A student in physic doth not satisfy himself to read over a system or body of physic, but he falls upon practicing physic: the life-blood of religion lies in the practice part. So, in the text: "He shall read" in the book of the law "all the days of his life: that he may learn to keep all the words of this law and these statutes, to do them" (Deuteronomy 17:19). Christians should be walking Bibles. Xenophon said, "Many read Lycurgus's laws, but few observe them." The word written is not only a rule of knowledge, but a rule of obedience: it is not only to mend our sight, but to mend our pace. David calls God's word "a lamp unto his feet" (Psalm 119:105). It was not only a light to his eyes to see by, but to his feet to walk by. By practice we trade the talent of knowledge, and turn it to profit. This is a blessed reading of scripture, when we fly from the sins which the word forbids, and espouse the duties which the word commands. Reading without practice will be but a torch to light men to hell.

DIRECTION XXII. *Make use of Christ's prophetical office.*--He is "the Lion of the tribe of Judah," to whom it is given "to open the book" of God, "and to loose the seven seals thereof"

(Revelation 5:5). Christ doth so teach as He doth quicken. "I am the light of the world: He that followeth me shall have," *lumen vitae*, "the light of life" (John 8:12). The philosopher saith, "Light and heat increase together." It is true here: where Christ comes into the soul with his light, there is the heat of spiritual life going along with it. Christ gives us *spiritualem gustum*, "a taste of the word": "Thou has taught me. How sweet are thy words unto my taste!" (Psalm 119:102,103). It is one thing to read a promise, another thing to "taste" it. Such as would be scripture-proficient, let them get Christ to be their teacher. "Then opened He their understanding, that they might understand the scriptures" (Luke 24:45). Christ did not only open the scriptures, but "opened their understanding".

DIRECTION XXIII. *Trend often upon the threshold of the sanctuary.*--Wait diligently on a rightly-constituted ministry: "Blessed is the man that heareth me, watching diligently at my gates, waiting at the posts of my doors" (Proverbs 8:34). Ministers are God's interpreters; it is their work to expound and open dark places of scripture. We read of their work to expound and open dark places of scripture. We read of "pitchers, and lamps within the pitchers" (Judges 7:16). Ministers are "earthen" pitchers (2 Corinthians 4:7). But these pitchers have lamps within them, to light souls in the dark.

DIRECTION XXIV. *Pray that God will make you profit.*-- "I am the Lord thy God, which teacheth thee to profit" (Isaiah 48:17). Make David's prayer: "Open Thou mine eyes, that I may behold wondrous things out of Thy law" (Psalm 119:18). Pray to God to take off the veil on the scripture, that you may understand it; and the veil on your heart, that you may believe it. Pray that God will not only give you His word as a *rule* of holiness, but His grace as a *principle* of holiness. Implore the guidance of God's Spirit: "Thou gavest them Thy good Spirit to instruct them" (Nehemiah 9:20). Though the ship hath a compass to sail by, and store of tackling, yet without a gale of wind it cannot sail. Though we have the word written as our compass to sail by, and make use of our endeavours as the tackling, yet, unless the Spirit of God blow upon us, we cannot sail with profit. When the Almighty is as "dew" unto us, then we "grow as the lily," and our "beauty is as the olive-tree" (Hosea 14:5,6). Beg the anointing of the Holy Ghost (see 1 John 2:20). One may see the figures on a dial, but he cannot tell how the day goes unless the sun shine: we may read many truths in the Bible, but we cannot know them savingly till God's Spirit shine in our souls (see 2 Corinthians 4:16). The Spirit is "a Spirit of wisdom and revelation" (Ephesians 1:17). When Philip joined himself to the eunuch's chariot, then he understood scripture (see Acts 8:29-35). When God's Spirit joins Himself to the word, then it will be effectual to salvation.

These rules observed, the word written would, through God's blessing, be "an engrafted word" (James 1:21). A good scion grafted into a bad stock changeth the nature of it, and makes it bear sweet and generous fruit; so when the word is grafted savingly into men's hearts, it doth sanctify them, and make them bring forth the sweet "fruits of righteousness" (Philippians 1:11).

Thus I have answered this question, *How we may read the scriptures with most spiritual profit.*

I shall conclude all with two corollaries:--

1. *Content not yourselves with the bare reading of scripture, but labour to find some spiritual increment and profit.*--Get the word transcribed into your hearts: "The law of his God is in his heart" (Psalm 37:31). Never leave till you are assimilated into the word. Such as profit by reading of the book of God are the best Christians alive; they answer God's cost, they credit religion, they save their souls.

2. *You who have profited by reading the holy scriptures, adore God's distinguishing grace.*--Bless God that He hath not only brought the light to you, but opened your eyes to see it; that He hath unlocked His hid treasure, and enriched you with saving knowledge. Some perish by *not having* scripture, and others by *not improving* it. That God should pass by millions in the world, and the lot of his electing love should fall upon you; that the scripture, like the pillar of cloud, should have a dark side to others, but a light side to you; that to others it should be a "dead letter," but to you the "savour of life"; that Christ should not only be revealed *to* you, but *in* you (see Galatians 1:16); how should you be in an holy ecstasy of wonder, and wish that you had hearts of seraphim burning in love to God, and the voices of angels, make heaven ring with God's praises!

OBJECTION. But some of the godly may say, they fear they do not profit by the word they read.

RESPONSE. As in the body, when there is a lipothymy or "fainting of the vital spirits", cordials are applied: so let me apply a few diving cordials to such as are ready to faint under the fear of non-proficiency.

1. *You may profit by reading the word, though you come short of others.*--The ground which brought forth but thirty-fold was "good ground" (Matthew 13:8). Say not you are non-proficients, because you do not go in equipage with other eminent saints: those were counted strong men among David's worthies, though they did not attain to the honour of the first three (see 2 Samuel 23:19,22,23).

2. *You may profit by reading the word, though you are not of so quick apprehension.*--Some impeach themselves of non-proficiency, because they are but slow of understanding. When our blessed Savior foretold His sufferings, the apostles themselves "understood not, and it was hid from them" (Luke

9:45). The author to the Hebrews speaks of some who were "dull of hearing" (Hebrews 5:11); yet they belonged to election. Such as have weaker judgments may have stronger affections. Leah was tender-eyed, yet fruitful. A Christian's intellectuals may be less quick and penetrating, yet that little knowledge he hath of scripture keeps him from sin; as a man that hath but weak sight, yet it keeps him from falling into the water.

3. *You may profit by reading scripture, though you have not so excellent memories.*--Many complain their memories leak. Christian, art thou grieved thou canst remember no more? Then, for thy comfort,

(1.) *Thou mayest have a good heart, though thou hast not so good a memory.*

(2.) *Though thou canst not remember all thou readest, yet thou rememberest that which is most material, and which thou hast most need of.*--At a feast we do not eat of every dish, but we take so much as nourisheth. It is with a good Christian's memory as it is with a lamp: though the lamp be not full of oil, yet it hath so much oil as makes the lamp burn: though thy memory be not full of scripture, yet thou retainest so much as makes thy love to God burn. Then be of good comfort; thou dost profit by what thou readest; and take notice of that encouraging scripture: "The Comforter, which is the Holy Ghost, He shall bring all things to your remembrance" (John 14:26).

Bible Reading: Why and How

J. C. Ryle

Search the scriptures—John 5:39
How readest thou?—Luke 10:26

Next to praying there is nothing so important in practical religion as Bible-reading. God has mercifully given us a book which is "able to make us wise unto salvation through faith which is in Christ Jesus" (2 Timothy 3:15). By reading that book we may learn what to believe, what to be, and what to do; how to live with comfort, and how to die in peace. Happy is that man who possesses a Bible! Happiest of all is he who not only reads it, but obeys it, and makes it the rule of his faith and practice!

Nevertheless it is a sorrowful fact that man has an unhappy skill in abusing God's gifts. His privileges, and power, and faculties, are all ingeniously perverted to other ends than those for which they were bestowed. His speech, his imagination, his intellect, his strength, his time, his influence, his money—instead of being used as instruments for glorifying his Maker—are generally wasted, or employed for his own selfish ends. And just as man naturally makes a bad use of his other mercies, so he does of the written Word. One sweeping charge may be brought against the whole of Christendom, and that charge is neglect and abuse of the Bible.

To prove this charge we have no need to look abroad: the proof lies at our own doors. I have no doubt that there are more Bibles in Great Britain at this moment than there ever were since the world began. There is more Bible buying and Bible selling—more Bible printing and Bible distributing—than ever was since England was a nation. We see Bibles in every bookseller's shop—Bibles of every size, price, and style—Bibles great, and Bibles small—Bibles for the rich, and Bibles for the poor. There are Bibles in almost every house in the land. But all this time I fear we are in danger of forgetting, that to have the Bible is one thing, and to read it quite another.

This neglected Book is the subject about which I address the readers of this paper today. Surely it is no light matter what you are doing with the Bible. Surely, when the plague is abroad, you should search and see whether the plague-spot is on you. Give me your attention while *I supply you with a few plain reasons why everyone who cares for his soul ought to value the Bible highly,* to study it regularly, and to make himself thoroughly acquainted with its contents.

I. In the first place, *there is no book in existence written in such a manner as the Bible.*

The Bible was "given by inspiration of God" (2 Timothy 3:16). In this respect it is utterly unlike all other writings. God taught the writers of it what to say. God put into their minds thoughts and ideas. God guided their pens in setting down those thoughts and ideas. When you read it, you are not reading the self-taught compositions of poor imperfect men like yourself, but the words of the eternal God. When you hear it, you are not listening to the erring opinions of short-lived mortals, but to the unchanging mind of the King of kings. The men who were employed to indite the Bible, spoke not of themselves. They "spake as they were moved by the Holy Ghost" (2 Peter 1:21). All other books in the world, however good and useful in their way, are more or less defective. The more you look at them the more you see their defects and blemishes. The Bible alone is absolutely perfect. From beginning to end it is "the Word of God."

I shall not waste time by attempting any long and laboured proof of this. I say boldly, that the Book itself is the best witness of its own inspiration. It is utterly inexplicable and unaccountable in any other point of view. It is the greatest standing miracle in the world. He that dares to say the Bible is not inspired, let him give a reasonable account of it, if he can. Let him explain the peculiar nature and character of the Book in a way that will satisfy any man of common sense. The burden of proof seems to my mind to lie on him.

It proves nothing against inspiration, as some have asserted, that the writers of the Bible have each a different style. Isaiah does not write like Jeremiah, and Paul does not write like John. This is perfectly true—and yet the works of these men are not a whit less equally inspired. The waters of the sea have many different shades. In one place they look blue, in another green. And yet the difference is owing to the depth or shallowness of the part we see, or to the nature of the bottom. The water in every case is the same salt sea. The breath of a man may produce different sounds, according to the character of the instrument on which he plays. The flute, the pipe, and the trumpet, have each their peculiar note. And yet the breath that calls forth the notes, is in each case one and the same. The light of the planets we see in heaven is very various, Mars, and Saturn, and Jupiter, have each a peculiar colour. And yet we know that the light of the sun, which each planet reflects, is in each case the one and the same. Just in the same way the books of the Old and New Testaments are all inspired truth, and yet the aspect of that truth varies according to the mind through which the Holy Ghost makes it flow. The handwriting and style of the writers differ enough to prove that each had a distinct individual being; but the Divine Guide who dictates and directs the whole is always one. All is alike inspired. Every chapter, and verse, and word, is from God.

Oh, that men who are troubled with doubts, and questions, and skeptical thoughts about inspiration, would calmly examine the Bible for themselves! Oh, that they would act on the advice which was the first step to Augustine's conversion—"Take it up and read it!—take it up and read it!" How many Gordian knots this course of action would cut! How many difficulties and objections would vanish away at once like mist before the rising sun! How many would soon confess, "The finger of God is here! God is in this Book, and I knew it not."

This is the Book about which I address the readers of this paper. Surely it is no light matter what you are doing with this Book. It is no light thing that God should have caused this Book to be "written for your learning," and that you should have before you "the oracles of God" (Romans 15:4; 3:2). I charge you, I summon you to give an honest answer to my question. What art thou doing with the Bible?—Dost thou read it at all?—HOW READEST THOU?

II. In the second place, *there is no knowledge absolutely needful to a man's salvation, except a knowledge of the things which are to be found in the Bible.*

We live in days when the words of Daniel are fulfilled before our eyes:—"Many run to and fro, and knowledge is increased" (Daniel 12:4). Schools are multiplying on every side. New colleges are set up. Old universities are reformed and improved. New books are continually coming forth. More is being taught—more is being learned—more is being read—than there ever was since the world began. It is all well. I rejoice at it. An ignorant population is a perilous and expensive burden to any nation. It is a ready prey to the first Absalom, or Catiline, or Wat Tyler, or Jack Cade, who may arise to entice it to do evil. But this I say— we must never forget that all the education a man's head can receive, will not save his soul from hell, unless he knows the truths of the Bible.

A man may have prodigious learning, and yet never be saved. He may be master of half the languages spoken round the globe. He may be acquainted with the highest and deepest things in heaven and earth. He may have read books till he is like a walking encyclopedia. He may be familiar with the stars of heaven— the birds of the air—the beasts of the earth, and the fishes of the sea. He may be able, like Solomon, to "speak of trees, from the cedar of Lebanon to the hyssop that grows on the wall, of beasts also, and fowls, and creeping things, and fishes" (1 Kings 4:33). He may be able to discourse of all the secrets of fire, air, earth, and water. And yet, if he dies ignorant of Bible truths, he dies a miserable man! Chemistry never silenced a guilty conscience. Mathematics never healed a broken heart. All the sciences in the world never smoothed down a dying pillow. No earthly philosophy ever supplied hope in death. No natural theology ever gave peace in the prospect of meeting a holy God. All these things are of the earth, earthly, and can never raise a man above the earth's level. They may enable a man to strut and fret his little season here below with a more dignified gait than his fellow-mortals, but they can never give him wings, and enable him to soar towards heaven. He that has the largest share of them, will find at length that without Bible knowledge he has got no lasting possession. Death will make an end of all his attainments, and after death they will do him no good at all.

A man may be a very ignorant man, and yet be saved. He may be unable to read a word, or write a letter. He may know nothing of geography beyond the bounds of his own parish, and be utterly unable to say which is nearest to England, Paris or New York. He may know nothing of arithmetic, and not see any difference between a million and a thousand. He may know nothing of history, not even of his own land, and be quite ignorant whether his country owes most to Semiramis, Boadicea, or Queen Elizabeth. He may know nothing of the affairs of his own times, and be incapable of telling you whether the Chancellor of the Exchequer, or the Commander-in-Chief, or the Archbishop of Canterbury is managing the national finances. He may know nothing of science and its discoveries—and whether Julius Caesar won his victories with gunpowder, or the apostles had a printing press, or the sun goes round the earth, may be matters about which he has not an idea. And yet if that very man has heard Bible truth with his ears, and believed it with his heart, he knows enough to save his soul. He will be found at last with Lazarus in Abraham's bosom, while his scientific fellow-creature, who has died unconverted, is lost forever.

There is much talk in these days about science and "useful knowledge." But after all a knowledge of the Bible is the one knowledge that is needful and eternally useful. A man may get to heaven without money, learning, health, or friends— but without Bible knowledge he will never get there at all. A man may have the mightiest of minds, and a memory stored with all that mighty mind can grasp— and yet, if he does not know the things of the Bible, he will make shipwreck of his soul for ever. Woe! woe! woe to the man who dies in ignorance of the Bible!

This is the Book about which I am addressing the readers of these pages today. It is no light matter what you do with such a book. It concerns the life of your soul. I summon you—I charge you to give an honest answer to my question. What are you doing with the Bible? Dost thou read it? HOW READEST THOU?

III. In the third place, *no book in existence contains such important matter as the Bible.*

The time would fail me if I were to enter fully into all the great things which are to be found in the Bible, and only in the Bible. It is not by any sketch or outline that the treasures of the Bible can be displayed. It would be easy to fill this volume with a list of the peculiar truths it reveals, and yet the half of its riches would be left untold.

How glorious and soul-satisfying is the description it gives us of God's plan of salvation, and the way by which our sins can be forgiven! The coming into the world of Jesus Christ, the God-man, to save sinners—the atonement He has made by suffering in our stead, the just for the unjust—the complete payment He has made for our sins by His own blood—the justification of every sinner who simply believes on Jesus—the readiness of Father, Son, and Holy Ghost, to receive, pardon, and save to the uttermost—how unspeakably grand and cheering are all these truths! We should know nothing of them without the Bible.

How comforting is the account it gives us of the Great Mediator of the New Testament—the man Christ Jesus! Four times over His picture is graciously drawn before our eyes. Four separate witnesses tell us of His miracles and His ministry— His sayings and His doings—His life and His death—His power and His love— His kindness and His patience—His ways, His words, His works, His thoughts, His heart. Blessed be God, there is one thing in the Bible which the most prejudiced reader can hardly fail to understand, and that is the character of Jesus Christ!

How encouraging are the examples the Bible gives us of good people! It tells us of many who were of like passions with ourselves—men and women who had cares, crosses, families, temptations, afflictions, diseases, like ourselves—and yet "by faith and patience inherited the promises," and got safe home (Hebrews 6:12). It keeps back nothing in the history of these people. Their mistakes, their infirmities, their conflicts, their experience, their prayers, their praises, their useful lives, their happy deaths—all are fully recorded. And it tells us the God and Saviour of these men and women still wants to be gracious and is altogether unchanged.

How instructive are the examples the Bible gives us of bad people! It tells us of men and women who had light, and knowledge, and opportunities, like ourselves, and yet hardened their hearts, loved the world, clung to their sins, would have their own way, despised reproof, and ruined their own souls forever. And it warns us that the God who punished Pharaoh, and Saul, and Ahab, and Jezebel, and Judas, and Ananias and Sapphira, is a God who never alters, and that there is a hell.

How precious are the promises which the Bible contains for the use of those who love God! There is hardly any possible emergency or condition for which it has not some "word in season." And it tells men that God loves to be put in remembrance of these promises, and that if He has said He will do a thing, His promise shall certainly be performed.

How blessed are the hopes which the Bible holds out to the believer in Christ Jesus! Peace in the hour of death—rest and happiness on the other side of the grave—a glorious body in the morning of the resurrection—a full and triumphant acquittal in the day of judgment—an everlasting reward in the kingdom of Christ—a joyful meeting with the Lord's people in the day of gathering together; these, these are the future prospects of every true Christian. They are all written in the Book—in the Book which is all true.

How striking is the light which the Bible throws on the character of man! It teaches us what men may be expected to be and do in every position and station of life. It gives us the deepest insight into the secret springs and motives of human actions, and the ordinary course of events under the control of human agents. It is the true "discerner of the thoughts and intents of the heart" (Hebrews 4:12). How deep is the wisdom contained in the books of Proverbs and Ecclesiastes! I can well understand an old divine saying, "Give me a candle and a Bible, and shut me up in a dark dungeon, and I will tell you all that the whole world is doing."

All these are things which men could find nowhere except in the Bible. We have probably not the least idea how little we should know about these things if we had not the Bible. We hardly know the value of the air we breathe, and the sun which shines on us, because we have never known what it is to be without them. We do not value truths on which I have been just now dwelling, because we do not realize the darkness of men to whom these truths have not been revealed. Surely no tongue can fully tell the value of the treasures this one volume contains. Well might old John Newton say that some books were copper books in his estimation, some were silver, and some few were gold—but the Bible alone was like a book all made up of bank notes.

This is the Book about which I address the reader of this paper this day. Surely it is no light matter what you are doing with the Bible. It is no light matter in what way you are using this treasure. I charge you, I summon you to give an honest answer to my question, What art thou doing with the Bible? Dost thou read it? HOW READEST THOU?

IV. In the fourth place, *no book in existence has produced such wonderful effects on mankind at large as the Bible.*

(a) This is the Book whose doctrines turned the world upside down in the days of the Apostles.

Eighteen centuries have now passed since God sent forth a few Jews from a remote corner of the earth, to do a work which according to man's judgment must have seemed impossible. He sent them forth at a time when the whole world was full of superstition, cruelty, lust, and sin. He sent them forth to proclaim that the established religions of the earth were false and useless and must be forsaken. He sent them forth to persuade men to give up old habits and customs and to live different lives. He sent them forth to do battle with the most groveling idolatry, with the vilest and most disgusting immorality, with vested interests, with old associations, with a bigoted priesthood, with sneering philosophers, with an ignorant population, with bloody-minded emperors, with the whole influence of Rome. Never was there an enterprise to all appearance more quixotic, and less likely to succeed!

And how did He arm them for this battle? He gave them no carnal weapons. He gave them no worldly power to compel assent, and no worldly riches to bribe belief. He simply put the Holy Ghost into their hearts, and the Scriptures into their hands. He simply bade them to expound and explain, to enforce and to publish the doctrines of the Bible. The preacher of Christianity in the first century was not a man with a sword and an army, to frighten people, like Muhammad, or a man with a license to be sensual, to allure people, like the priests of the shameful idols of Hinduism. No! He was nothing more than one holy man with one holy book.

And how did these men of one book prosper? In a few generations they entirely changed the face of society by the doctrines of the Bible. They emptied the temples of the heathen gods. They famished idolatry, left it high and dry like a stranded ship. They brought into the world a higher tone of morality between man and man. They raised the character and position of woman. They altered the standard of purity and decency. They put an end to many cruel and bloody customs, such as the gladiatorial fights. There was no stopping the change. Persecution and opposition were useless. One victory after another was won. One bad thing after another melted away. Whether men liked it or not, they were insensibly affected by the movement of the new religion and drawn within the whirlpool of its power. The earth shook, and their rotten refuges fell to the ground. The flood rose, and they found themselves obliged to rise with it. The tree of Christianity swelled and grew, and the chains they cast round it to arrest its growth snapped like tow. And all this was done by the doctrines of the Bible. Talk of victories indeed! What are the victories of

Alexander, and Caesar, and Marlborough, and Napoleon, and Wellington, compared with those I have just mentioned? For extent, for completeness, for results, for permanence, there are no victories like the victories of the Bible.

(b) This is the Book which turned Europe upside down in the days of the glorious Protestant Reformation.

No man can read the history of Christendom as it was five hundred years ago and not see that darkness covered the whole professing Church of Christ, even a darkness that might be felt. So great was the change which had come over Christianity, that if an apostle had risen from the dead he would not have recognized it and would have thought that heathenism had revived again. The doctrines of the Gospel lay buried under a dense mass of human traditions. Penances, pilgrimages, and indulgences, relic-worship and image-worship, saint worship and worship of the Virgin Mary formed the sum and substance of most people's religion. The Church was made an idol. The priests and ministers of the Church usurped the place of Christ. And by what means was all this miserable darkness cleared away? By none so much as by bringing forth once more the Bible.

It was not merely the preaching of Luther and his friends that established Protestantism in Germany. The grand lever which overthrew the Pope's power in that country was Luther's translation of the Bible into the German tongue. It was not merely the writings of Cranmer and the English Reformers which cast down popery in England. The seeds of the work thus carried forward were first sown by Wycliffe's translation of the Bible many years before. It was not merely the quarrel of Henry VII and the Pope of Rome, which loosened the Pope's hold on English minds. It was the royal permission to have the Bible translated and set up in churches, so that everyone who liked might read it. Yes! It was the reading and circulation of Scripture which mainly established the cause of Protestantism in England, Germany, and Switzerland. Without it the people would probably have returned to their former bondage when the first reformers died. But by the reading of the Bible the public mind became gradually leavened with the principles of true religion. Men's eyes became thoroughly open. Their spiritual understandings became thoroughly enlarged. The abominations of popery became distinctly visible. The excellence of the pure Gospel became a rooted idea in their hearts. It was then in vain for Popes to thunder forth excommunications. It was useless for Kings and Queens to attempt to stop the course of Protestantism by fire and sword. It was all too late. The people knew too much. They had seen the light. They had heard the joyful sound. They had tasted the truth. The sun had risen on their minds. The scales had fallen from their eyes. The Bible had done its appointed work within them, and that work was not to be overthrown. The people would not return to Egypt. The clock could not be put back again. A mental and moral revolution had been effected, and mainly effected by God's Word. Those are the true revolutions which the Bible effects. What are all the revolutions which France and England have gone through compared to these? No revolutions are so bloodless, none so satisfactory, none so rich in lasting results, as the revolutions accomplished by the Bible!

This is the book on which the well-being of nations has always hinged, and with which the best interests of every nation in Christendom at this moment are inseparably bound up. Just in proportion as the Bible is honoured or not, light or darkness, morality or immorality, true religion or superstition, liberty or despotism, good laws or bad, will be found in a land. Come with me and open the pages of history, and you will read the proofs in time past. Read it in the history of Israel under the Kings. How great was the wickedness that then prevailed! But who can wonder? The law of the Lord had been completely lost sight of, and was found in the days of Josiah thrown aside in a corner of the temple (2 Kings 22:8). Read it in the history of the Jews in our Lord Jesus Christ's time. How awful the picture of scribes and Pharisees, and their religion! But who can wonder? The Scripture was "made of none effect by man's traditions" (Matthew 15:6). Read it in the history of the Church of Christ in the middle ages. What can be worse than the accounts we have seen of its ignorance and superstition? But who can wonder? The times might well be dark, when men had not the light of the Bible.

This is the Book to which the civilized world is indebted for many of its best and most praiseworthy institutions. Few probably are aware how many are the good things that men have adopted for the public benefit, of which the origin may be clearly traced up to the Bible. It has left lasting marks wherever it has been received. From the Bible are drawn many of the best laws by which society is kept in order. From the Bible has been obtained the standard of morality about truth, honesty, and the relations of man and wife, which prevails among Christian nations, and which—however feebly respected in many cases—makes so great a difference between Christians and heathen. To the Bible we are indebted for that most merciful provision for the poor man, the Sabbath day. To the influence of the Bible we owe nearly every humane and charitable institution in existence. The sick, the poor, the aged, the orphan, the lunatic, the idiot, and the blind were seldom or never thought of before the Bible leavened the world. You may search in vain for any record of institutions for their aid in the histories of Athens or of Rome. Alas! There are many who sneer at the Bible and say the world would get on well enough without it, who little think how great are their own obligations to the Bible. Little does the infidel workman think, as he lies sick in some of our great hospitals, that he owes all his present comforts to the very book he affects to despise. Had it not been for the Bible, he might have died in misery, uncared for, unnoticed, and alone. Verily the world we live in is fearfully unconscious of its debts. The last day alone, I believe, will tell the full amount of benefit conferred upon it by the Bible.

This wonderful book is the subject about which I address the reader of this paper this day. Surely it is no light matter what you are doing with the Bible. The swords of conquering generals—the ship in which Nelson led the fleets of England to victory—the hydraulic press which raised the tubular bridge at the Menai—each and all of these are objects of interest as instruments of mighty power. The Book I speak of this day is an instrument a thousand fold mightier still. Surely it is no light matter whether you are paying it the attention it deserves. I charge you, I summon you to give me an honest answer this day—what are thou doing with the Bible? Dost thou read it? HOW READEST THOU?

V. In the fifth place, *no book in existence can do so much for everyone who reads it rightly as the Bible.*

The Bible does not profess to teach the wisdom of this world. It was not written to explain geology or astronomy. It will neither instruct you in mathematics, nor in natural philosophy. It will not make you a doctor, or a lawyer, or an engineer.

But there is another world to be thought of beside that world in which man now lives. There are other ends for which man was created beside making money and working. There are other interests which he is meant to attend to beside those of his body, and those interests are the interests of his soul. It is the interests of the immortal soul which the Bible is especially able to promote. If you would know law, you may study Blackstone or Sugden. If you would know astronomy or geology, you may study Herschel and Lyell. But if you would know how to have your soul saved, you must study the written Word of God.

The Bible is "able to make a man wise unto salvation, through faith which is in Christ Jesus" (2 Timothy 3:15). It can show you the way which leads to heaven. It can teach you everything you need to know, point out everything you need to believe, and explain everything you need to do. It can show you what you are— a sinner. It can show you what God is—perfectly holy. It can show you the great giver of pardon, peace, and grace—Jesus Christ. I have read of an Englishman who visited Scotland in the days of Blair, Rutherford, and Dickson, three famous preachers, and heard all three in succession. He said that the first showed him the majesty of God—the second showed him the beauty of Christ—and the third showed him all his heart. It is the glory and beauty of the Bible that it is always teaching these three things more or less, from the first chapter of it to the last.

The Bible applied to the heart by the Holy Ghost is the grand instrument by which souls are first converted to God. That mighty change is generally begun by some text or doctrine of the Word brought home to a man's conscience. In this way the Bible has worked moral miracles by thousands. It has made drunkards become sober—unchaste people become pure—thieves become honest—and violent-tempered people become meek. It has wholly altered the course of men's lives. It has caused their old things to pass away and made all their ways new. It has taught worldly people to seek first the kingdom of God. It has taught lovers of pleasure to become lovers of God. It has taught the stream of men's affections to run upwards instead of running downwards. It has made men think of heaven, instead of always thinking of earth, and live by faith, instead of living by sight. All this it has done in every part of the world. All this it is doing still. What are the Romish miracles which men believe, compared to all this, even if they were true? Those are the truly great miracles which are yearly worked by the Word.

The Bible applied to the heart by the Holy Ghost is the chief means by which men are built up and established in the faith after their conversion. It is able to cleanse them, to sanctify them, to instruct them in righteousness, and to furnish them thoroughly for all good works (Psalm 119:9; John 17:17; 2 Timothy 3:16, 17). The Spirit ordinarily does these things by the written Word; sometimes by the Word read, and sometimes by the Word preached, but seldom, if ever, without the Word. The Bible can show a believer how to walk in this world so as to please God. It can teach him to glorify Christ in all the relations of life and can make him a good master, servant, subject, husband, father, or son. It can enable him to bear afflictions and privations without murmuring and say, "It is well." It can enable him to look down into the grave and say, "I fear no evil" (Psalm 23:4). It can enable him to think on judgment and eternity and not feel afraid. It can enable him to bear persecution without flinching and to give up liberty and life rather than deny Christ's truth. Is he drowsy in soul? It can awaken him. Is he mourning? It can comfort him. Is he erring? It can restore him. Is he weak? It can make him strong. Is he in bad company? It can keep him from evil. Is he alone? It can talk with him (Proverbs 6:22). All this the Bible can do for all believers—for the least as well as the greatest—for the richest as well as the poorest. It has done it for thousands already and is doing it for thousands every day.

The man who has the Bible and the Holy Spirit in his heart, has everything which is absolutely needful to make him spiritually wise. He needs no priest to break the bread of life for him. He needs no ancient traditions, no writings of the Fathers, no voice of the Church to guide him into all truth. He has the well of truth open before him, and what can he want more? Yes! Though he be shut up alone in a prison, or cast on a desert island—though he never see a church, or minister, or sacrament again—if he has but the Bible, he has got the infallible guide and wants no other. If he has but the will to read that Bible rightly, it will certainly teach him the road that leads to heaven. It is here alone that infallibility resides. It is not in the Church. It is not in the Councils. It is not in ministers. It is only in the written Word.

(a) *I know well that many say they have found no saving power in the Bible.* They tell us they have tried to read it and have learned nothing from it. They can see in it nothing but hard and deep things. They ask us what we mean by talking of its power.

I answer that the Bible no doubt contains hard things, or else it would not be the book of God. It contains things hard to comprehend, but only hard because we have not grasp of mind to comprehend them. It contains things above our reasoning powers, but nothing that might not be explained if the eyes of our understanding were not feeble and dim. But is not an acknowledgment of our own ignorance the very cornerstone and foundation of all knowledge? Must not many things be taken for granted in the beginning of every science before we can proceed one step towards acquaintance with it? Do we not require our children to learn many things of which they cannot see the meaning at first? And ought we not then to expect to find "deep things" when we begin studying the Word of God, and yet to believe that if we persevere in reading it the meaning of many of them will one day be made clear? No doubt we ought so to expect and so to believe. We must read with humility. We must take much on trust. We must believe that what we know not now, we shall know hereafter—some part in this world, and all in the world to come.

But I ask that man who has given up reading the Bible because it contains hard things, whether he did not find many things in it easy and plain? I put it to his conscience whether he did not see great landmarks and principles in it all the way through? I ask him whether the things needful to salvation did not stand out boldly before his eyes, like the lighthouses on English headlands from Land's End to the mouth of the Thames. What should we think of the captain of a steamer who brought up at night in the entrance of the Channel, on the plea that he did not know every parish, and village, and creek, along the British coast. Should we not think him a lazy coward, when the lights on the Lizard, and Eddystone, and the Start, and Portland, and St. Catherine's, and Beachy Head, and Dungeness, and the Forelands, were shining forth like so many lamps to guide him up to the river? Should we not say, Why did you not steer by the great leading lights? And what ought we to say to the man who gives up reading the Bible because it contains hard things, when his own state, and the path to heaven, and the way to serve God, are all written down clearly and unmistakably, as with a sunbeam? Surely we ought to tell that man his objections are no better than lazy excuses and do not deserve to be heard.

(b) *I know well that many raise the objection that thousands read the Bible and are not a whit the better* for their reading. And they ask us, when this is the case, what becomes of the Bible's boasted power?

I answer that the reason why so many read the Bible without benefit is plain and simple—they do not read it in the right way. There is generally a right way and a wrong way of doing everything in the world; and just as it is with other things, so it is in the matter of reading the Bible. The Bible is not so entirely different from all other books as to make it of no importance in what spirit and manner you read it. It does not do good, as a matter of course, by merely running our eyes over the print, any more than the sacraments do good by mere virtue of our receiving them. It does not ordinarily do good, unless it is read with humility and earnest prayer. The best steam-engine that was ever built is useless if a man does not know how to work it. The best sundial that was ever constructed will not tell its owner the time of day if he is so ignorant as to put it up in the shade. Just as it is with that steam-engine, and that sundial, so it is with the Bible. When men read it without profit, the fault is not in the Book, but in themselves.

I tell the man who doubts the power of the Bible, because many read it and are no better for the reading, that the abuse of a thing is no argument against the use of it. I tell him boldly that never did man or woman read that book in a childlike persevering spirit—like the Ethiopian eunuch and the Bereans (Acts 8:28; 17:11)—and miss the way to heaven. Yes, many a broken cistern will be exposed to shame in the day of judgment; but there will not rise up one soul who will be able to say that he went thirsting to the Bible and found in it no living water—he searched for truth in the Scriptures, and searching did not find it. The words which are spoken of Wisdom in the Proverbs are strictly true of the Bible: "If thou criest after knowledge, and liftest up thy voice for understanding; if thou seekest her as silver, and searchest for her as for hid treasures; then shalt thou understand the fear of the Lord, and find the knowledge of God" (Proverbs 2:3-5).

This wonderful Book is the subject about which I address the readers of this paper this day. Surely it is no light matter what you are doing with the Bible. What should you think of the man who in time of cholera despised a sure recipe for preserving the health of his body? What must be thought of you if you despise the only sure recipe for the everlasting health of your soul? I charge you, I entreat you, to give an honest answer to my question. What dost thou do with the Bible?— Dost thou read it? HOW READEST THOU?

VI. In the sixth place, *the Bible is the only rule by which all questions of doctrine or of duty can be tried.*

The Lord God knows the weakness and infirmity of our poor fallen understandings. He knows that, even after conversion, our perceptions of right and wrong are exceedingly indistinct. He knows how artfully Satan can gild error with an appearance of truth and can dress up wrong with plausible arguments till it looks like right. Knowing all this, He has mercifully provided us with an unerring standard of truth and error, right and wrong, and has taken care to make that standard a written book—even the Scripture.

No one can look round the world and not see the wisdom of such a provision. No one can live long and not find out that he is constantly in need of a counselor and adviser—of a rule of faith and practice on which he can depend. Unless he lives like a beast without a soul and conscience, he will find himself constantly assailed by difficult and puzzling questions. He will be often asking himself: What must I believe and what must I do?

(a) The world is full of difficulties about points of doctrine. The house of error lies close alongside the house of truth. The door of one is so like the door of the other that there is continual risk of mistakes.

Does a man read or travel much? He will soon find the most opposite opinions prevailing among those who are called Christians. He will discover that different persons give the most different answers to the important question, What shall I do to be saved? The Roman Catholic and the Protestant—the

Neologian and the Tractarian—the Mormonite and the Swedenborgian—each and all will assert that he alone has the truth. Each and all will tell him that safety is only to be found in his party. Each and all say, "Come with us." All this is puzzling. What shall a man do?

Does he settle down quietly in some English or Scotch parish? He will soon find that even in our own land the most conflicting views are held. He will soon discover that there are serious differences among Christians as to the comparative importance of the various parts and articles of the faith. One man thinks of nothing but Church government—another of nothing but sacraments, services, and forms— a third of nothing but preaching the Gospel. Does he apply to ministers for a solution? He will perhaps find one minister teaching one doctrine and another another. All this is puzzling. What shall a man do?

There is only one answer to this question. A man must make the Bible alone his rule. He must receive nothing and believe nothing, which is not according to the Word. He must try all religious teaching by one simple test—Does it square with the Bible? What saith the Scripture?

I would to God the eyes of the laity of this country were more open on this subject. I would to God they would learn to weigh sermons, books, opinions, and ministers in the scales of the Bible and to value all according to their conformity to the Word. I would to God they would see that it matters little who says a thing—whether he be Father or Reformer—Bishop or Archbishop—Priest or Deacon—Archdeacon or Dean. The only question is: Is the thing said Scriptural? If it is, it ought to be received and believed. If it is not, it ought to be rejected and cast aside. I fear the consequences of that servile acceptance of everything which "the parson" says, which is so common among many English laymen. I fear lest they be led they know not whither, like the blinded Syrians, and awake some day to find themselves in the power of Rome (2 Kings 6:20). Oh, that men in England would only remember for what purpose the Bible was given them!

I tell the English laymen that it is nonsense to say, as some do, that it is presumptuous to judge a minister's teaching by the Word. When one doctrine is proclaimed in one parish and another in another, people must read and judge for themselves. Both doctrines cannot be right, and both ought to be tried by the Word. I charge them, above all things, never to suppose that any true minister of the Gospel will dislike his people measuring all he teaches by the Bible. On the contrary, the more they read the Bible and prove all he says by the Bible, the better he will be pleased. A false minister may say, "You have no right to use your private judgment: leave the Bible to us who are ordained." A true minister will say, "Search the Scriptures, and if I do not teach you what is Scriptural, do not believe me." A false minister may cry, "Hear the Church," and "Hear me." A true minister will say, "Hear the Word of God."

(b) But the world is not only full of difficulties about points of doctrine: it is equally full of difficulties about points of practice. Every professing Christian, who wishes to act conscientiously must know that it is so. The most puzzling questions are continually arising. He is tried on every side by doubts as to the line of duty and can often hardly see what is the right thing to do.

He is tried by questions connected with the management of his worldly calling, if he is in business or in trade. He sometimes sees things going on of a very doubtful character—things that can hardly be called fair, straightforward, truthful, and doing as you would be done by. But then everybody in the trade does these things. They have always been done in the most respectable houses. There would be no carrying on a profitable business if they were not done. They are not things distinctly named and prohibited by God. All this is very puzzling. What is a man to do?

He is tried by questions about worldly amusements. Races and dances, operas and theatres, and card parties are all very doubtful methods of spending time. But then he sees numbers of great people taking part in them. Are all these people wrong? Can there really be such mighty harm in these things? All this is very puzzling. What is a man to do?

He is tried by questions about the education of his children. He wishes to train them up morally and religiously and to remember their souls. But he is told by many sensible people that young persons will be young—that it does not do to check and restrain them too much, and that he ought to attend pantomimes and children's parties and give children's dances himself. He is informed that this nobleman, or that lady of rank, always does so, and yet they are reckoned religious people. Surely it cannot be wrong. All this is very puzzling. What is he to do?

There is only one answer to all these questions. A man must make the Bible his rule of conduct. He must make its leading principles the compass by which he steers his course through life. By the letter or spirit of the Bible he must test every difficult point and question. "To the law and to the testimony! What saith the Scripture?" He ought to care nothing for what other people may think right. He ought not to set his watch by the clock of his neighbour, but by the sundial of the Word.

I charge my readers solemnly to act on the maxim I have just laid down and to adhere to it rigidly all the days of their lives. You will never repent of it. Make it a leading principle never to act contrary to the Word. Care not for the charge of over-strictness and needless precision. Remember you serve a strict and holy God. Listen not to the common objection that the rule you have laid down is impossible and cannot be observed in such a world as this. Let those who make such an objection speak out plainly and tell us for what purpose the Bible was given to man. Let them remember that by the Bible we shall all be judged at the last day, and let them learn to judge themselves by it here, lest they be judged and condemned by it hereafter.

This mighty rule of faith and practice is the book about which I am addressing the readers of this paper this day. Surely it is no light matter what you are doing with the Bible. Surely when danger is abroad on the right hand and on the left, you should consider what you are doing with the safeguard which God has provided. I charge you, I beseech you, to give an honest answer to my question. What art thou doing with the Bible? Dost thou read it? HOW READEST THOU?

VII. In the seventh place, *the Bible is the book which all true servants of God have always lived on and loved.*

Every living thing which God creates requires food. The life that God imparts needs sustaining and nourishing. It is so with animal and vegetable life—with birds, beasts, fishes, reptiles, insects, and plants. It is equally so with spiritual life. When the Holy Ghost raises a man from the death of sin and makes him a new creature in Christ Jesus, the new principle in that man's heart requires food, and the only food which will sustain it is the Word of God.

There never was a man or woman truly converted, from one end of the world to the other, who did not love the revealed will of God. Just as a child born into the world desires naturally the milk provided for its nourishment, so does a soul "born again" desire the sincere milk of the Word. This is a common mark of all the children of God—they "delight in the law of the Lord" (Psalm 1:2).

Show me a person who despises Bible reading or thinks little of Bible preaching, and I hold it to be a certain fact that he is not yet "born again." He may be zealous about forms and ceremonies. He may be diligent in attending sacraments and daily services. But if these things are more precious to him than the Bible, I cannot think he is a converted man. Tell me what the Bible is to a man, and I will generally tell you what he is. This is the pulse to try—this is the barometer to look at—if we would know the state of the heart. I have no notion of the Spirit dwelling in a man and not giving clear evidence of His presence. And I believe it to be a signal evidence of the

Spirit's presence when the Word is really precious to a man's soul.

Love to the Word is one of the characteristics we see in Job. Little as we know of this patriarch and his age, this at least stands out clearly. He says, "I have esteemed the words of His mouth more than my necessary food" (Job 23:12).

Love to the Word is a shining feature in the character of David. Mark how it appears all through that wonderful part of Scripture, Psalm 119. He might well say, "Oh, how I love thy law!" (Psalm 119:97).

Love to the Word is a striking point in the character of St. Paul. What were he and his companions but men "mighty in the Scriptures?" What were his sermons but expositions and applications of the Word?

Love to the Word appears pre-eminently in our Lord and Saviour Jesus Christ. He read it publicly. He quoted it continually. He expounded it frequently. He advised the Jews to "search" it. He used it as His weapon to resist the devil. He said repeatedly, "The Scripture must be fulfilled." Almost the last thing He did was to "open the understanding of His disciples, that they might understand the Scriptures" (Luke 24:45). I am afraid that man can be no true servant of Christ, who has not something of his Master's mind and feelings towards the Bible.

Love to the Word has been a prominent feature in the history of all the saints, of whom we know anything, since the days of the Apostles. This is the lamp which Athanasius and Chrysostom and Augustine followed. This is the compass which kept the Waldensians and Albigenses from making shipwreck of the faith. This is the well which was reopened by Wycliffe and Luther, after it had been long stopped up. This is the sword with which Latimer, Jewell, and Knox won their victories. This is the manna which fed Baxter and Owen and the noble host of the Puritans and made them strong to battle. This is the armoury from which Whitfield and Wesley drew their powerful weapons. This is the mine from which Bickersteth and M'Cheyne brought forth rich gold. Differing as these holy men did in some matters, on one point they were all agreed—they all delighted in the Word.

Love to the Word is one of the first things that appears in the converted heathen at the various missionary stations throughout the world. In hot climates and in cold—among savage people and among civilized—in New Zealand, in the South Sea Islands, in Africa, in India—it is always the same. They enjoy hearing it read. They long to be able to read it themselves. They wonder why Christians did not send it to them before. How striking is the picture which Moffat draws of Airicaner, the fierce South African chieftain, when first brought under the power of the Gospel! "Often have I seen him," he says, "under the shadow of a great rock nearly the live-long day, eagerly perusing the pages of the Bible! He said, "It is never old and never cold." How affecting was the language of another old Negro, when some would have dissuaded him from learning to read because of his great age. "No!" he said, "I will never give it up till I die. It is worth all the labour to be able to read that one verse, 'God so loved the world, that he gave his only begotten Son that whosoever believeth in him should not perish, but have eternal life.'"

Love to the Bible is one of the grand points of agreement among all converted men and women in our own land. Episcopalians and Presbyterians, Baptists and

Independents, Methodists and Plymouth Brethren—all unite in honouring the Bible as soon as they are real Christians. This is the manna which all the tribes of our Israel feed upon and find satisfying food. This is the fountain round which no sheep goes away thirsty. Oh, that believers in this country would learn to cleave more closely to the written Word! Oh, that they would see that the more the Bible, and the Bible only, is the substance of men's religion, the more they agree! It is probable there never was an uninspired book more universally admired than Bunyan's *The Pilgrim's Progress.* It is a book where all denominations of Christians delight to honour. It has won praise from all parties. Now what a striking fact it is that the author was pre-eminently a man of one book! He had read hardly anything but the Bible.

It is a blessed thought that there will be "much people" in heaven at last. Few as the Lord's people undoubtedly are at any one given time or place, yet all gathered together at last, they will be "a multitude that no man can number" (Revelation 19:1; 7:9). They will be of one heart and mind. They will have passed through like experience. They will all have repented, believed, lived holy, prayerful, and humble. They will all have washed their robes and made them white in the blood of the Lamb. But one thing beside all this they will have in common: they will all love the texts and doctrines of the Bible. The Bible will have been their food and delight in the days of their pilgrimage on earth. And the Bible will be a common subject of their joyful meditation and retrospect when they are gathered together in heaven.

This Book, which all true Christians live upon and love, is the subject about which I am addressing the readers of this paper this day. Surely it is no light matter what you are doing with the Bible. Surely it is matter for serious inquiry, whether you know anything of this love to the

Word and have this mark of walking "in the footsteps of the flock" (Song of Solomon 1:8). I charge you, I entreat you to give me an honest answer. What art thou doing with the Bible? Dost thou read it? HOW READEST THOU?

VIII. In the last place, *the Bible is the only book which can comfort a man in the last hours of his life.*

Death is an event which in all probability is before us all. There is no avoiding it. It is the river which each of us must cross. I who write, and you who read, have each one day to die. It is good to remember this. We are all sadly apt to put away the subject from us. "Each man thinks each man mortal but himself." I want everyone to do his duty in life, but I also want everyone to think of death. I want everyone to know how to live, but I also want everyone to know how to die.

Death is a solemn event to all. It is the winding up of all earthly plans and expectations. It is a separation from all we have loved and lived with. It is often accompanied by much bodily pain and distress. It brings us to the grave, the worm, and corruption. It opens the door to judgment and eternity—to heaven or to hell. It is an event after which there is no chance or space for repentance. Other mistakes may be corrected or retrieved but not a mistake on our deathbeds. As the tree falls, there it must lie. No conversion in the coffin! No new birth after we have ceased to breathe! And death is before us all. It may be close at hand. The time of our departure is quite uncertain. But sooner or later we must each lie down alone and die. All these are serious considerations.

Death is a solemn event even to the believer in Christ. For him no doubt the "sting of death" is taken away

(1 Corinthians 15:55). Death has become one of his privileges, for he is Christ's. Living or dying, he is the Lord's. If he lives, Christ lives in him; if he dies, he goes to live with Christ. To him "to live is Christ, and to die is gain" (Philippians 1:21). Death frees him from many trials—from a weak body, a corrupt heart, a tempting devil, and an ensnaring or persecuting world. Death admits him to the enjoyment of many blessings. He rests from his labours; the hope of a joyful resurrection is changed into a certainty—he has the company of holy redeemed spirits—he is "with Christ." All this is true—and yet, even to a believer, death is a solemn thing. Flesh and blood naturally shrink from it. To part from all we love is a wrench and trial to the feelings. The world we go to is a world unknown, even though it is our home. Friendly and harmless as death is to a believer, it is not an event to be treated lightly. It always must be a very solemn thing.

It becomes every thoughtful and sensible man to consider calmly how he is going to meet death. Gird up your loins, like a man, and look the subject in the face. Listen to me, while I tell you a few things about the end to which we are coming.

The good things of the world cannot comfort a man when he draws near death. All the gold of California and Australia will not provide light for the dark valley. Money can buy the best medical advice and attendance for a man's body; but money cannot buy peace for his conscience, heart, and soul.

Relatives, loved friends, and servants cannot comfort a man when he draws near death. They may minister affectionately to his bodily wants. They may watch by his bedside tenderly and anticipate his every wish. They may smooth down his dying pillow and support his sinking frame in their arms. But they cannot "minister to a mind diseased." They cannot stop the achings of a troubled heart. They cannot screen an uneasy conscience from the eye of God.

The pleasures of the world cannot comfort a man when he draws near death. The brilliant ballroom—the merry dance—the midnight revel—the party of Epsom races—the card table—the box at the opera—the voices of singing men and singing women—all these are at length distasteful things. To hear of hunting and shooting engagements gives him no pleasure. To be invited to feasts, regattas, and garden parties gives him no ease. He cannot hide from himself that these are hollow, empty, powerless things. They jar upon the ear of his conscience. They are out of harmony with his condition. They cannot stop one gap in his heart, when the last enemy is coming in like a flood. They cannot make him calm in the prospect of meeting a holy God.

Books and newspapers cannot comfort a man when he draws near death. The most brilliant writings of Macaulay or Dickens will pall on his ear. The most able article in the *Times* will fail to interest him. *Punch* and the *Illustrated London News* and the last new novel will lie unopened and unheeded. Their time will be past. Their vocation will be gone. Whatever they may be in health, they are useless in the hour of death.

There is but one fountain of comfort for a man drawing near to his end, and that is the Bible. Chapters taken out of the Bible—texts out of the Bible—statements of truth taken out of the Bible—books containing matter drawn from the Bible—these are a man's only chance of comfort when he comes to die. I do not at all say that the Bible will do good, as a matter of course, to a dying man, if he has not valued it before. I know, unhappily, too much of deathbeds to say that. I do not say whether it is probable that he who has been unbelieving and neglectful of the Bible in life will at once believe and get comfort from it in death. But I do say positively that no dying man will ever get real comfort, except from the contents of the Word of God. All comfort from any other source is a house built upon sand.

I lay this down as a rule of universal application. I make no exception in favour of any class on earth. Kings and poor men, learned and unlearned—all are on a level in this matter. There is not a jot of real consolation for any dying man unless he gets it from the Bible. Chapters, passages, texts, promises, and doctrines of Scripture—heard, received, believed, and rested on—these are the only comforters I dare promise to anyone when he leaves the world. Taking the sacrament will do a man no more good than the Popish extreme unction, so long as the Word is not received and believed. Priestly absolution will no more ease the conscience than the incantations of a heathen magician, if the poor dying sinner does not receive and believe Bible truth. I tell everyone who reads this paper, that although men may seem to get on comfortably without the Bible while they live, they may be sure that without the Bible they cannot comfortably die. It was a true confession of the learned Selden—"There is no book upon which we can rest in a dying moment but the Bible."

I might easily confirm all I have just said by examples and illustrations. I might show you the deathbeds of men who have affected to despise the Bible. I might tell you how Voltaire and Paine, the famous infidels, died in misery, bitterness, rage, fear, and despair. I might show you the happy deathbeds of those who have loved the Bible and believed it, and the blessed effect the sight of their deathbeds had on others. Cecil—a minister whose praise ought to be in all churches—says, "I shall never forget standing by the bedside of my dying mother. 'Are you afraid to die?' I asked. 'No!' she replied. 'But why does the uncertainty of another state give you no concern?' 'Because God has said, "Fear not; when thou passest through the waters I will be with thee, and through the rivers, they shall not overflow thee"' (Isaiah 43:2). I might easily multiply illustrations of this kind. But I think it better to conclude this part of my subject by giving the results of my own observations as a minister.

I have seen not a few dying persons in my time. I have seen great varieties of manner and deportment among them. I have seen some die sullen, silent, and comfortless. I have seen others die ignorant, unconcerned, and apparently without much fear. I have seen some die so wearied out with long illness that they were quite willing to depart, and yet they did not seem to me at all in a fit state to go before God. I have seen others die with professions of hope and trust in God, without leaving satisfactory evidences that they were on the rock. I have seen others die who, I believe, were "in Christ," and safe, and yet they never seemed to enjoy much sensible comfort. I have seen some few dying in the full assurance of hope and, like Bunyan's "Standfast," giving glorious testimony to Christ's faithfulness, even in the river. But one thing I have never seen. I never saw anyone enjoy what I should call real, solid, calm, reasonable peace on his deathbed, who did not draw his peace from the Bible. And this I am bold to say, that the man who thinks to go to his death-bed without having the Bible for his comforter, his companion, and his friend is one of the greatest madmen in the world. There are no comforts for the soul but Bible comforts, and he who has not got hold of these has got hold of nothing at all, unless it be a broken reed.

The only comforter for a deathbed is the book about which I address the readers of this paper this day. Surely it is no light matter whether you read that book or not. Surely a dying man, in a dying world, should seriously consider whether he has got anything to comfort him when his turn comes to die. I charge you, I entreat you, for the last time, to give an honest answer to my question. What art thou doing with the Bible? Dost thou read it? HOW READEST THOU?

I have now given the reasons why I press on every reader the duty and importance of reading the Bible. I have shown that no book is written in such a manner as the Bible, that knowledge of the Bible is absolutely necessary to salvation, that no book contains such matter, that no book has done so much for the world generally, that no book can do so much for everyone who reads it aright, that this book is the only rule of faith and practice, that it is, and always has been, the food of all true servants of God, and that it is the only book which can comfort men when they die. All these are ancient things. I do not pretend to tell anything new. I have only gathered together old truths and tried to mould them into a new shape. Let me finish all by addressing a few plain words to the conscience of every class of readers.

(1) *This paper may fall into the hands of some who can read, but never do read the Bible at all.* Are you one of them? If you are, I have something to say to you.

    I cannot comfort you in your present state of mind. It would be mockery and deceit to do so. I cannot speak to you of peace and heaven, while you treat the Bible as you do. You are in danger of losing your soul.

You are in danger, because your neglected Bible is a plain evidence that you do not love God. The health of a man's body may generally be known by his appetite. The health of a man's soul may be known by his treatment of the Bible. Now you are manifestly labouring under a sore disease. Will you not repent?

I know I cannot reach your heart. I cannot make you see and feel these things. I can only enter my solemn protest against your present treatment of the Bible and lay that protest before your conscience. I do so with all my soul. Oh, beware lest you repent too late! Beware lest you put off reading the Bible till you send for the doctor in your last illness and then find the Bible a sealed book, and dark as the cloud between the hosts of Israel and Egypt to your anxious soul! Beware lest you go on saying all your life, "Men do very well without all this Bible-reading," and find at length, to your cost, that men do very ill and end in hell! Beware lest the day come when you will feel, "Had I but honoured the Bible as much as I have honoured the newspaper, I should not have been left without comfort in my last hours!" Bible-neglecting reader, I give you a plain warning. The plague cross is at present on your door. The Lord have mercy upon your soul!

(2) *This paper may fall into the hands of someone who is willing to begin reading the Bible but wants advice on the subject.* Are you that man? Listen to me, and I will give you a few short hints.

(a) For one thing, *begin reading your Bible this very day.* The way to do a thing is to do it, and the way to read the Bible is actually to read it. It is not meaning, or wishing, or resolving, or intending, or thinking about it which will advance you one step. You must positively read. There is no royal road in this matter any more than in the matter of prayer. If you cannot read yourself, you must persuade somebody else to read to you. But one way or another, through eyes or ears, the words of Scripture must actually pass before your mind.

(b) For another thing, *read the Bible with an earnest desire to understand it.* Think not for a moment that the great object is to turn over a certain quantity of printed paper, and that it matters nothing whether you understand it or not. Some ignorant people seem to fancy that all is done if they clear off so many chapters every day, though they may not have a notion what they are all about and only know that they have pushed on their mark so many leaves. This is turning Bible reading into a mere form. It is almost as bad as the Popish habit of buying indulgences, by saying an almost fabulous numbers of avemarias and paternosters. It reminds one of the poor Hottentot who ate up a Dutch hymnbook because he saw it comforted his neighbours' hearts. Settle it down in your mind as a general principle that a Bible not understood is a Bible that does no good. Say to yourself often as you read, "What is all this about?" Dig for the meaning like a man digging for Australian gold. Work hard, and do not give up the work in a hurry.

(c) For another thing, *read the Bible with childlike faith and humility.* Open your heart as you open your book, and say, "Speak, Lord, for thy servant heareth." Resolve to believe implicitly whatever you find there, however much it may run counter to your own prejudices. Resolve to receive heartily every statement of truth whether you like it or not. Beware of that miserable habit of mind into which some readers of the Bible fall. They receive some doctrines because they like them: they reject others because they are condemning to themselves or to some love, relation, or friend. At this rate the Bible is useless. Are we to be judges of what ought to be in the Word? Do we know better than God? Settle it down in your mind that you will receive all and believe all, and that what you cannot understand you will take on trust. Remember, when you pray, you are speaking to God, and God hears you. But remember, when you read, God is speaking to you, and you are not to "answer again," but to listen.

(d) For another thing, *read the Bible in a spirit of obedience and self-application.* Sit down to the study of it with a daily determination that you will live by its rules, rest on its statements, and act on its commands. Consider, as you travel through every chapter, "How does this affect my position and course of conduct? What does this teach me?" It is poor work to read the Bible from mere curiosity and for speculative purposes in order to fill your head and store your mind with opinions, while you do not allow the book to influence your heart and life. That Bible is read best which is practiced most.

(e) For another thing, *read the Bible daily.* Make it a part of every day's business to read and meditate on some portion of God's Word. Private means of grace are just as needful every day for our souls as food and clothing are for our bodies. Yesterday's bread will not feed the labourer today, and today's bread will not feed the labourer tomorrow. Do as the Israelites did in the wilderness. Gather your manna fresh every morning. Choose your own seasons and hours. Do not scramble over and hurry your reading. Give your Bible the best and not the worst part of your time. But whatever plan you pursue, let it be a rule of your life to visit the throne of grace and the Bible every day.

(f) For another thing, *read all the Bible, and read it in an orderly way.* I fear there are many parts of the Word which some people never read at all. This is to say the least, a very presumptuous habit. "All Scripture is profitable" (2 Timothy 3:16). To this habit may be traced that want of broad, well-proportioned views of truth, which is so common in this day. Some people's Bible-reading is a system of perpetual dipping and picking. They do not seem to have an idea of regularly going through the whole book. This also is a great mistake. No doubt in times of sickness and affliction it is allowable to search out seasonable portions. But with this exception, I believe it is by far the best plan to begin the Old and New Testaments at the same time—to read each straight through to the end, and then begin again. This is a matter in which every one must be persuaded in his own mind. I can only say it has been my own plan for nearly forty years, and I have never seen cause to alter it.

(g) For another thing, *read the Bible fairly and honestly.* Determine to take everything in its plain, obvious meaning and regard all forced interpretations with great suspicion. As a general rule, whatever a verse of the Bible seems to mean, it does mean. Cecil's rule is a very valuable one—"The right way of interpreting Scripture is to take it as we find it, without any attempt to force it into any particular system. "Well," said Hooker, "I hold it for a most infallible rule in the exposition of Scripture, that when a literal construction will stand, the furthest from the literal is commonly the worst."

(h) In the last place, *read the Bible with Christ continually in view.* The grand primary object of all Scripture is to testify of Jesus. Old Testament ceremonies are shadows of Christ. Old Testament history shows the world's need of Christ. Old Testament prophecies are full of Christ's suffering, and of Christ's glory yet to come. The first advent and the second—the Lord's humiliation and the Lord's kingdom—the cross and the crown, shine forth everywhere in the Bible. Keep fast hold on this clue, if you would read the Bible aright.

I might easily add to these hints, if space permitted. Few and short as they are, you will find them worth attention. Act upon them, and I firmly believe you will never be allowed to miss the way to heaven. Act upon them, and you will find light continually increasing in your mind. No book of evidence can be compared with that internal evidence which he obtains who daily uses the Word in the right way. Such a man does not need the books of learned men. He has the witness in himself. The book satisfies and feeds his soul. A poor Christian woman once said to an infidel, "I am no scholar. I cannot argue like you. But I know that honey is honey, because it leaves a sweet taste in my mouth. And I know the Bible to be God's book, because of the taste it leaves in my heart."

(3) *This paper may fall into the hands of someone who loves and believes the Bible, and yet reads it but little.* I fear there are many such in this day. It is a day of bustle and hurry. It is a day of talking, and committee meetings, and public work. These things are all very well in their way, but I fear that they sometimes clip and cut short the private reading of the Bible. Does your conscience tell you that you are one of the persons I speak of? Listen to me, and I will say a few things which deserve your serious attention.

You are the man that is likely to get little comfort from the Bible in time of need. Trial is a sifting season. Affliction is a searching wind, which strips the leaves off the trees and brings to light the bird's nests. Now I fear that your stores of Bible consolations may one day run very low. I fear lest you should find yourself at last on very short allowance and come into harbour weak, worn and thin.

You are the man that is likely never to be established in the truth. I shall not be surprised to hear that you are troubled with doubts and questionings about assurance, grace, faith, perseverance, and the like. The devil is an old and cunning enemy. Like the Benjamites, he can "throw stones at a hair-breadth, and not miss" (Judges 20:16). He can quote Scripture readily enough when he pleases. Now you are not sufficiently ready with your weapons to be able to fight a good fight with him. Your armour does not fit you well. Your sword sits loosely in your hand.

You are the man that is likely to make mistakes in life. I shall not wonder if I am told that you have erred about your own marriage, erred about your children's education—erred about the conduct of your household—erred about the company you keep. The world you steer through is full of rocks, shoals, and sandbanks. You are not sufficiently familiar either with the lights or charts.

You are the man that is likely to be carried away by some specious false teacher for a season. It will not surprise me if I hear that someone of those clever, eloquent men, who can "make the worse appear the better cause," is leading you into many follies. You are wanting in ballast. No wonder if you are tossed to and fro, like a cork on the waves.

All these are uncomfortable things. I want every reader of this paper to escape them all. Take the advice I offer you this day. Do not merely read your Bible "a little," but read it a great deal. "Let the Word of Christ dwell in you richly" (Colossians 3:16). Do not be a mere babe in spiritual knowledge. Seek to become well instructed in the kingdom of heaven," and to be continually adding new things to old. A religion of feeling is an uncertain thing. It is like the tide, sometimes high, and sometimes low. It is like the moon, sometimes bright, and sometimes dim. A religion of deep Bible knowledge is a firm and lasting possession. It enables a man not merely to say, "I feel hope in

Christ," but "I know whom I have believed" (2 Timothy 1:12).

(4) *This paper may fall into the hands of someone who reads the Bible much, and yet fancies he is no better for his reading.* This is a crafty temptation of the devil. At one stage he says, "Do not read the Bible at all." At another he says, "Your reading does you no good: give it up." Are you that man? I feel for you from the bottom of my soul. Let me try to do you good.

Do not think you are getting no good from the Bible, merely because you do not see that good day by day. *The greatest effects are by no means those which make the most noise and are most easily observed. The greatest effects are often silent, quiet, and hard to detect at the time they are being produced.* Think of the influence of the moon upon the earth and of the air upon human lungs. Remember how silently the dew falls and how imperceptibly the grass grows. There may be far more doing than you think in your soul by your Bible-reading.

The Word may be gradually producing deep impressions on your heart, of which you are not at present aware. Often when the memory is retaining no facts, the character of a man is receiving some everlasting impression. Is sin becoming every year more hateful to you? Is Christ becoming every year more precious? Is holiness becoming every year more lovely and desirable in your eyes? If these things are so, take courage. The Bible is doing you good, though you many not be able to trace it out day by day.

The Bible may be restraining you from sin or delusion into which you would otherwise run. It may be daily keeping you back, and hedging you up, and preventing many a false step. Ah, you might soon find this out to your cost, if you were to cease reading the Word! The very familiarity of blessings sometimes makes us insensible to their value. Resist the devil. Settle it down in your mind as an established rule, that, whether you feel it at the moment or not, you are inhaling spiritual health by reading the Bible, and insensibly becoming more strong.

(5) *This paper may fall into the hands of some who really love the Bible, live upon the Bible, and read it much.* Are you one of these? Give me your attention, and I will mention a few things which we shall do well to lay to heart for time to come.

Let us resolve to read the Bible more and more every year we live. Let us try to get it rooted in our memories and engrafted into our hearts. Let us be thoroughly well provisioned with it against the voyage of death. Who knows but we may have a very stormy passage? Sight and hearing may fail us, and we may be in deep waters. Oh, to have the Word "hid in our hearts" in such an hour as that! (Psalm 119:11).

Let us resolve to be more watchful over our Bible-reading every year that we live. Let us be jealously careful about the time we give to it, and the manner that time is spent. Let us beware of omitting our daily reading without sufficient cause. Let us not be gaping, and yawning, and dozing over our book while we read. Let us read like a London merchant studying the industrial columns in the *Times*—or like a wife reading a husband's letter from a distant land. Let us be very careful that we never exalt any minister, or sermon, or book, or tract, or friend above the Word. Cursed be that book, or tract, or human counsel, which creeps in between us and the Bible, and hides the Bible from our eyes! Once more I say, let us be very watchful. The moment we open the Bible the devil sits down by our side. Oh, to read with a hungry spirit and a simple desire for edification!

Let us resolve to honour the Bible more in our families. Let us read it morning and evening to our children and households and not be ashamed to let men see that we do so. Let us not be discouraged by seeing no good arise from it. The Bible-reading in a family has kept many a one from the goal and the workhouse, if it has not kept him from hell.

Let us resolve to meditate more on the Bible. It is good to take with us two or three texts when we go out into the world and to turn them over and over in our minds whenever we have a little leisure. It keeps out many vain thoughts. It clenches the nail of daily reading. It preserves our souls from stagnating and breeding corrupt things. It sanctifies and quickens our memories and prevents them becoming like those ponds where the frogs live but the fish die.

Let us resolve to talk more to believers about the Bible when we meet them. Alas, the conversation of Christians, when they do meet, is often sadly unprofitable. How many frivolous, trifling, and uncharitable things are said! Let us bring out the Bible more, and it will help to drive the devil away and keep our hearts in tune. Oh, that we may all strive so to walk together in this evil world, that Jesus may often draw near and go with us, as He went with the two disciples journeying to Emmaus!

Last of all, *let us resolve to live by the Bible more and more every year we live.* Let us frequently take account of all our opinions and practices, of our habits and tempers, of our behavior in public and in private—in the world and by our own firesides. Let us measure all by the Bible and resolve, by God's help, to conform to it. Oh that we may learn increasingly to "cleanse our ways" by the Word! (Psalm 119:9).

How to Read the Bible

Charles H. Spurgeon

Have ye not read? . . . Have ye not read? . . .
If ye had known what this meaneth.—
Matthew 12:3-7.

The scribes and Pharisees were great readers of the law. They studied the sacred books continually, pouring over each word and letter. They made notes of very little importance, as to which was the middle verse of the entire Old Testament, which verse was halfway to the middle, and how many times such a word occurred, and even how many time a letter occurred, and the size of the letter, and its peculiar position. They have left us a mass of notes upon the mere words of Holy Scripture. They might have done the same thing to another book for that matter, and the information would have been about as important as the facts which they have so industriously collected concerning the letter of the Old Testament.

They were, however, intense readers of the law. They picked a quarrel with the Saviour over a matter touching this law, for they carried it at their fingers' ends and were ready to use it as a bird of prey does its talon to tear and rend. Our Lord's disciples had plucked some ears of corn and rubbed them between their hands. According to Pharisaic interpretation, to rub an ear of corn is a kind of threshing, and, as it is very wrong to thresh on the Sabbath day, therefore it must be very wrong to rub out an ear or two of wheat when you are hungry on the Sabbath morning. That was their argument, and they came to the Saviour with it and with their version of the Sabbath law. The Saviour generally carried the war into the enemy's camp, and He did so on this occasion. He met them on their own ground, and He said to them, "Have ye not read?"—a cutting question to the scribes and Pharisees, though there is nothing apparently sharp about it. It was a very fair and proper question to put to them; but only think of putting it to them. "Have ye not read?" "Read!" they could have said, "Why, we have read the book through very many times. We are always reading it. No passage escapes our critical eyes." Yet our Lord proceeded to put the question a second time—"Have ye not read?" as if they had not read after all, though they were the greatest readers of the law then living. He insinuated that they had not read at all; and then He gave them incidentally the reason why He had asked them whether they had read. He said, "If ye had known what this meaneth," as much as to say, "You have not read, because you have not understood. Your eyes have gone over the words, and you have counted the letters, and you have marked the position of each verse and word, and you have said learned things about all the books, and yet you are not even readers of the sacred volume, for you have not acquired the true art of reading; you do not understand, and therefore you do not truly read it. You are mere skimmers and glancers at the Word: you have not read it, for you do not understand it." That is the first point of our present discourse.

I. *Understand What You Are Reading*

I scarcely need to preface these remarks by saying that *we must read the Scriptures.* You know how necessary it is that we should be fed upon the truth of Holy Scripture. Need I suggest the question as to whether you do read your Bibles or not? I am afraid that this is a magazine reading age, a newspaper reading age, a periodical reading age, but not so much a Bible reading age as it ought to be. In the old times men used to have a scant supply of other literature, but they found a library enough in the one book, the Bible. And how they did read the Bible!

How little of Scripture there is in modern sermons compared with the sermons of those masters of theology, the Puritan divines! Almost every sentence of theirs seems to cast side lights upon a text of Scripture; not only the one they are preaching about, but many others as well are set in a new light as the discourse proceeds. I would to God that we ministers kept more closely to thc grand old Book. We should be instructive preachers if we did so, even if we were ignorant of "modern thought," and were not "abreast of the times."

As for you who have not to preach, *the best food for you is the Word of God itself.* Sermons and books are well enough, but streams that run for a long distance above ground gradually gather for themselves somewhat of the soil through which they flow, and they lose the cool freshness with which they started from the spring head. It is always best to drink at the well and not from the tank. You shall find that reading the Word of God for yourselves, reading it rather than notes upon it, is the surest way of growing in grace. Drink of the unadulterated milk of the Word of God, and not of the skim milk, or the milk and water of man's word.

Our point is that *much apparent Bible reading is not Bible reading at all.* The verses pass under the eye, and the sentences glide over the mind, but there is no true reading. An old preacher used to say, the Word has mighty free course among many nowadays, for it goes in at one of their ears and out at the other; so it seems to be with some readers—they can read a very great deal, because they do not read anything. The eye glances but the mind never rests. The soul does not light upon the truth and stay there. It flits over the landscape as a bird might do, but it builds no nest and finds not rest for the sole of its foot. Such reading is not reading. Understanding the meaning is the essence of true reading. Reading has a kernel to it, and the mere shell is worth little.

In prayer there is such a thing as praying in prayer—a praying that is the heart of the prayer. So in praise there is a praising in song, an inward fire of intense devotion which is the life of the hallelujah. It is even so with the reading of the Scriptures. *There is an interior reading, a kernel reading—a true and living reading of the Word.* This is the soul of reading; and, if it be not there, the reading is a mechanical exercise and profits nothing.

Unless we understand what we read we have not read it; the heart of the reading is absent. We commonly condemn the Romanists for keeping the daily service in the Latin tongue; yet it might as well be in the Latin language as in any other tongue if it is not understood by the people. Some comfort themselves with the idea that they have done a good action when they have read a chapter, into the meaning of which they have not entered at all; but does not nature herself reject this as a mere superstition. If you had turned the book upside down, and spent the same time in looking at the characters in that direction, you would have gained as much good from it as you will in reading it in the regular way without understanding it. If you had a New Testament in Greek it would be very Greek to some of you, but it would do you as much good to look at that as it does to look at the English New Testament unless you read it with an understanding heart.

It is not the letter which saves the soul; the letter kills in many senses, and never can it give life. If you harp on the letter alone you may be tempted to use it as a weapon against the truth, as the Pharisees did of old, and your knowledge of the letter may breed pride in you to your destruction. It is the spirit, the real inner meaning, that is sucked into the soul, by which we are blessed and sanctified. We become saturated with the Word of God, like Gideon's fleece; and this can only come to pass by our receiving it into our minds and hearts, accepting it as God's truth, and so far understanding it as to delight in it. We must understand it, then, or else we have not read it aright.

Certainly *the benefit of reading must come to the soul by the way of the understanding.* There must be knowledge of God before there can be love to God: there must be a knowledge of divine things as they are revealed, before there can be an enjoyment of them. We must try to make out, as far as our finite minds can grasp it, what God means by this and what He means by that; otherwise we may kiss the Book and have no love to its contents, we may reverence the letter and yet really have no devotion towards the Lord who speaks to us in these words. You will never get comfort to your soul out of what you do not understand, nor find guidance for your life out of what you do not comprehend; nor can any practical bearing upon your character come out of that which is not understood by you.

Alert Minds

If we are thus to understand what we read or otherwise we read in vain, this shows us that when we come to the study of Holy Scripture *we should try to have our mind well awake to it.* We are not always fit, it seems to me, to read the Bible. At times it were well for us to stop before we open the volume. "Put off thy shoe from thy foot, for the place whereon thou standest is holy ground." You have just come in from careful thought and anxiety about your worldly business, and you cannot immediately take that Book and enter into its heavenly mysteries. As you ask a blessing over your meal before you fall to, so it would be a good rule for you to ask a blessing on the Word before you partake of its heavenly food. Pray the Lord to strengthen your eyes before you dare to look into the eternal light of Scripture. Scripture reading is our spiritual meal time. *Sound the gong and call in every faculty to the Lord's own table to feast upon the precious meat which is now to be partaken of;* or, rather, ring the church bell as for worship, for the studying of the Holy Scripture ought to be as solemn a deed as when we worship in the Lord's house.

Meditation on the Word

If these things be so, you will see at once that, if you are to understand what you read, *you will need to meditate upon it. Some passages of Scripture lie clear before us—blessed shallows in which the lambs may wade; but there are deeps in which our mind might rather drown herself than swim with pleasure,* if she came there without caution. There are texts of Scripture which are made and constructed on purpose to make us think. By this means, among others, our heavenly Father would educate us for heaven—by making us think our way into divine mysteries. Hence He puts the Word in a somewhat involved form to compel us to meditate upon it before we reach the sweetness of it. He might have explained it to us so that we might catch the thought in a minute, but He does not please to do so in every case. Many of the veils which are cast over Scripture are not meant to hide the meaning from the diligent but to compel the mind to be active, for often the diligence of the heart in seeking to know the divine mind does the heart more good than the knowledge itself. Meditation and careful thought exercise us and strengthen the soul for the reception of the yet more lofty truths.

We must meditate. These grapes will yield no wine till we tread upon them. These olives must be put under the wheel, and pressed again and again, that the oil may flow therefrom. In a dish of nuts, you may know which nut has been eaten, because there is a little hole which the insect has punctured through the shell—just a little hole, and then inside there is the living thing eating up the kernel. Well, it is a grand thing to bore through the shell of the letter, and then to live inside feeding upon the kernel. I would wish to be such a little worm as that, living within and upon the Word of God, having bored my way through the shell, and having reached the innermost mystery of the blessed gospel. The Word of God is always most precious to the man who most lives upon it.

As I sat last year under a wide-spreading beech, admiring that most wonderful of trees, I thought to myself, I do not think half as much of this beech tree as the squirrel does. I see him leap from bough to bough, and I feel sure that he dearly values the old beech tree, because he has his home somewhere inside it in a hollow place, these branches are his shelter, and those beech nuts are his food. He lives upon the tree. It is his world, his playground, his granary, his home; indeed, it is everything to him, and it is not so to me, for I find my rest and food elsewhere. With God's Word it is well for us to be like squirrels living in it and living on it. Let us exercise our minds by leaping from bough to bough of it, find our rest and food in it, and make it our all in all. We shall be the people that get the profit out of it if we make it to be our food, our medicine, our treasury, our armoury, our rest, our delight. May the Holy Ghost lead us to do this and make the Word precious to our souls.

Prayer to Its Author

I would next remind you that for this end we shall be compelled to pray. *It is a grand thing to be driven to think, it is a grander thing to be driven to pray through having been made to think.* Am I not addressing some of you who do not read the Word of God, and am I not speaking to many more who do read it, but do not read it with the strong resolve that they will understand it? I know it must be so. Do you wish to begin to be true readers? Then you must get to your knees. You must cry to God for direction. Who understands a book best? The author of it.

If I want to ascertain the real meaning of a rather twisted sentence, and the author lives near me, and I can call upon him, I shall ring at his door and say "Would you kindly tell me what you mean by that sentence? I have no doubt whatever that it is very clear, but I am such a simpleton, that I cannot make it out. I have not the knowledge and grasp of the subject which you possess, and therefore your allusions and descriptions are beyond my range of knowledge. It is quite within your range, and commonplace to you, but it is very difficult to me. Would you kindly explain your meaning to me?" A good man would be glad to be thus treated, and would think it no trouble to unravel his meaning to a candid inquirer. Thus I should be sure to get the correct meaning, for I should be going to the fountainhead when I consulted the author himself.

So, *the Holy Spirit is with us, and when we take His book and begin to read, and want to know what it means, we must ask the Holy Spirit to reveal the meaning.* He will not work a miracle, but He will elevate our minds, and He will suggest to us thoughts which will lead us on by their natural relation the one to the other, till at last we come to the pith and marrow of His divine instruction. Seek then very earnestly the guidance of the Holy Spirit, for if the very soul of reading be the understanding of what we read, then we must in prayer call upon the Holy Ghost to unlock the secret mysteries of the inspired Word.

Using Means and Helps

If we thus ask the guidance and teaching of the Holy Spirit, it will follow that we shall *be ready to use all means and helps towards the understanding of the Scriptures.* When Philip asked the Ethiopian eunuch whether he understood the prophecy of Isaiah he replied, "How can I, unless some man should guide me?" Then Philip went up and opened to him the Word of the Lord.

Some, under the pretence of being taught of the Spirit of God refuse to be instructed by books or by living men. This is no honouring of the Spirit of God; it is a disrespect to Him, for if *He gives to some of His servants more light than to others—and it is clear He does—then they are bound to give that light to others and to use it for the good of the Church.*

But if the other part of the Church refuse to receive that light, to what end did the Spirit of God give it? This would imply that there is a mistake somewhere in the economy of gifts and graces, which is managed by the Holy Spirit. It cannot be so. The Lord Jesus Christ pleases to give more knowledge of His Word and more insight into it to some of His servants than to others, and it is ours joyfully to accept the knowledge which He gives in such ways as He chooses to give it.

It would be most wicked of us to say, "We will not have the heavenly treasure which exists in earthen vessels. If God will give us the heavenly treasure out of His own hand, but not through the earthen vessel, we will have it. We think we are too wise, too heavenly minded, too spiritual altogether to care for jewels when they are placed in earthen pots. We will not hear anybody, and we will not read anything except the Book itself, neither will we accept any light, except that which comes in through a crack in our own roof. We will not see by another man's candle, we would rather remain in the dark." Brethren, do not let us fall into such folly. Let the light come from God, and though a child shall bring it, we will joyfully accept it. If any one of His servants, whether Paul or Apollos or Cephas, shall have received light from Him, behold, *"all are yours, and ye are Christ's, and Christ is God's," and therefore accept the light which God has kindled,* and ask for grace that you may turn that light upon the Word so that when you read it you may understand it.

I do not wish to say much more about this, but I should like to press it home upon some of you. You have Bibles at home, I know; you would not like to be without Bibles, you would think you were heathens if you had no Bibles. You have them very neatly bound, and they are very fine looking volumes: not much thumbed, not much worn, and not likely to be so, for they only come out on Sundays for an airing, and they lie in lavender with the clean pocket-handkerchiefs all the rest of the week. You do not read the Word, you do not search it, and how can you expect to get the divine blessing? If the heavenly gold is not worth digging for, you are not likely to discover it. Often and often have I told you that the searching of the Scriptures is not the way of salvation. The Lord has said, "Believe in the Lord Jesus Christ, and thou shalt be saved." But still, the reading of the Word often leads, like the hearing of it, to faith, and faith brings salvation; for faith comes by hearing, and reading is a sort of hearing. While you are seeking to know what the gospel is, it may please God to bless your souls.

But what poor reading some of you give to your Bibles. I do not want to say anything which is too severe because it is not strictly true—let your own consciences speak—but still, I make bold to enquire, Do not many of you read the Bible in a very hurried way—just a little bit, and off you go? Do you not soon forget what you have read, and lose what little effect it seemed to have? How few of you are resolved to get at its soul, its juice, its life, its essence, and to drink in its meaning. If you do not do that, I tell you again your reading is miserable reading, dead reading, unprofitable reading; it is not reading at all, the name would be misapplied. May the Spirit give you repentance touching this thing.

II. *Seek Out the Spiritual Teaching*

I think that is in my text, because our Lord says, "Have ye not read?" Then again, "Have ye not read?" and then He says, "If ye had known what this meaneth"—and the meaning is something very spiritual. The text He quoted was, "I will have mercy, and not sacrifice," a text out of prophet Hosea. The scribes and Pharisees were all for the letter, the sacrifice, the killing of the bullock, and so on. They overlooked the spiritual meaning of the passage, "I will have mercy, and not sacrifice"—namely, that God prefers that we should care for our fellow creatures rather than that we should observe any ceremonial of His law, so as to cause hunger or thirst, and thereby death, to any of the creatures that His hands have made. They ought to have passed beyond the outward into the spiritual, and all our reading ought to do the same.

Notice that this should be the case when we read the historical passages. "Have ye not read what David did, when he was an hungered, and they that were with him; how he entered into the house of God, and did eat the shew bread, which was not lawful for him to eat, neither for them which were with him, but only for the priests?" This was a piece of history, and they ought to have read it as to have found spiritual instruction in it. I have heard very stupid people say, "Well, I do not care to read the historical parts of Scripture." Beloved friends, you do not know what you are talking about when you say so. I say to you now by experience that *I have sometimes found even a greater depth of spirituality in the histories than I have in the Psalms.* You will say, "How is that?" I assert that when you reach the inner and spiritual meaning of a history you are often surprised at the clearness—the realistic force—with which the teaching comes home to your soul.

Some of the most marvelous mysteries of revelation are better understood by being set before our eyes in the histories than they are by the verbal declaration of them. When we have the statement to explain the illustration, the illustration expands and vivifies the statement. For instance, when our Lord Himself would explain to us what faith was. He sent us to the history of the brazen serpent; and who that has ever read the story of the brazen serpent has not felt that he has had a better idea of faith through the picture of the dying snake-bitten persons looking to the serpent of brass and living, than from any description which even Paul has given us, wondrously as he defines and describes. Never depreciate the historical portions of God's Word, but when you cannot get good out of them, say, "That is my foolish head and my slow heart. O Lord, be pleased to clear my brain and cleanse my soul." When He answers that prayer you will feel that every portion of God's Word is given by inspiration and is and must be profitable to you. Cry, "Open thou mine eyes, that I may behold wondrous things out of thy law."

Just the same thing is true with regard to all the ceremonial precepts, because the Saviour goes on to say, "Have ye not read in the law, how that on the Sabbath days, the priests in the temple profane the Sabbath, and are blameless?" *There is not a single precept in the old law but has an inner sense and meaning:* therefore do not turn away from Leviticus, or say, "I cannot read these chapters in the Books of Exodus and Numbers. They are all about the tribes and their standards, the stations in the wilderness and the halts of the march, the tabernacle and furniture, or about golden knops and bowls, and boards, and sockets, and precious stones, and blue and scarlet and fine linen." No, but look for the inner meaning. Make thorough search; for as in a king's treasure that which is the most closely locked up and the hardest to come at is the choicest jewel of the treasure, so is it with the Holy Scriptures.

Did you ever go to the British Museum library? There are many books of reference there which the reader is allowed to take down when he pleases. There are other books for which he must write a ticket, and he cannot get them without the ticket; but they have certain choice books which you will not see without a special order, and then there is an unlocking of doors, and an opening of cases, and there is a watcher with you while you make your inspection. You are scarcely allowed to put your eye on the manuscript, for fear you should blot a letter out by glancing at it; it is such a precious treasure; there is not another copy of it in all the world, and so you cannot get at it easily. Just so, *there are choice and precious doctrines of God's Word which are locked up in such cases as Leviticus or Solomon's Song, and you cannot get at them without a deal of unlocking of doors; and the Holy Spirit Himself must be with you, or else you will never come at the priceless treasure.* The higher truths are as choicely hidden away as the precious regalia of princes; therefore search as well as read. Do not be satisfied with a ceremonial precept till you reach its spiritual meaning, for that is true reading. You have not read till you understand the spirit of the matter.

It is just the same with the doctrinal statements of God's Word. I have sorrowfully observed some persons who are very orthodox, and who can repeat their creed very glibly, and yet the principal use that they make of their orthodoxy is to sit and watch the preacher with the view of framing a charge against him. He has uttered a single sentence which is judged to be half a hair's breadth below the standard. "That man is not sound. He said some good things, but he is rotten at the core, I am certain. He used an expression which was not eighteen ounces to the pound." Sixteen ounces to the pound are not enough for these dear brethren of whom I speak, they must have something more and over and above the shekel of the sanctuary. Their knowledge is used as a microscope to magnify trifling differences. I hesitate not to say that I have come across persons who

"Could a hair divide
Betwixt the west and north-west side"

in matters of divinity, but who know nothing about the things of God in their real meaning. They have never drank them into their souls, but only sucked them up into their mouths to spit them out on others. The doctrine of election is one thing, but to know that God has predestinated you, and to have the fruit of it in the good works to which you are ordained, is quite another thing. To talk about the love of Christ, to talk about the heaven that is provided for His people, and such things—all this is very well; but this may be done without any personal acquaintance with them. Therefore never be satisfied with a sound creed, but desire to have it graven on tablets of your heart. The doctrines of grace are good, but the grace of the doctrines is better still. See that you have it, and be not content with the idea that you are instructed until you so understand the doctrine that you have felt its spiritual power.

This makes us feel, that, in order to come to this, *we shall need to feel Jesus present with us whenever we read the Word.* Mark that fifth verse, which I would now bring before you, "Have ye not read in the law, how on the Sabbath days the priests in the temple profane the Sabbath, and are blameless? But I say unto you, That in this place is one greater than the temple." They thought much about the letter of the Word, but they did not know that He was there who is the Sabbath's Master—man's Lord and the Sabbath's Lord, and Lord of everything. When you have got hold of a creed, or of an ordinance, or anything that is outward in the letter, pray the Lord to make you feel that there is something greater than the printed book, and something better than the mere shell of the creed. There is one Person greater than them all, and to Him we should cry that He may be ever with us. O living Christ, make this a living word to me. Thy word is life, but not without the Holy Spirit. I may know this Book of Thine from beginning to end, and repeat it all from Genesis to Revelation, and yet it may be a dead book, and I may be a dead soul. But, Lord, be present here; then will I look up from the Book to the Lord; from the precept to Him who fulfilled it; from the law to Him who honoured it; from the threatening to Him who has borne it for me, and from the promise to Him in whom it is "Yea and amen." Then we shall read the Book so differently. He is here with me in this chamber of mine: I must not trifle. He leans over me, He puts His finger along the lines, I can see His pierced hand: I will read it as in His presence. I will read it, knowing that He is the substance of it—that He is the proof of this Book as well as the writer of it; the sum of this Scripture as well as the author of it. That is the way for true students to become wise. *You will get at the soul of Scripture when you can keep Jesus with you while you are reading.*

Did you never hear a sermon as to which you felt that if Jesus had come into that pulpit while the man was making his oration, He would have said, "Go down, go down; what business have you here? I sent you to preach about Me, and you preach about a dozen other things. Go home and learn of Me, and then come and talk." That sermon which does not lead to Christ, or of which Jesus Christ is not the top and the bottom, is a sort of sermon that will make the devils in hell to laugh, but might make the angels of God to weep, if they were capable of such emotion.

You remember the story of the Welshman who heard a young man preach a very fine sermon—a grand sermon, a highfaluting, spread-eagle sermon; and when he had done, he asked the Welshman what he thought of it. The man replied that he did not think anything of it. "And why not?" "Because there was no Jesus Christ in it." "Well," said he, "but my text did not seem to run that way." "Never mind," said the Welshman, "your sermon ought to run that way." "I do not see that," said the young man. "No," said the other, "you do not see how to preach yet. This is the way to preach. From every little village in England— it does not matter where it is—there is sure to be a road to London. Though there may not be a road to certain other places, there is certain to be a road to London. Now, from every text in the Bible there is a road to Jesus Christ, and the way to preach is just to say, 'How can I get from this text to Jesus Christ?' and then go preaching all the way along it." "But," said the young man, "suppose I find a text that has not got a road to Jesus Christ?" "I have preached for forty years," said the old man, "and I have never found such a Scripture, but if I ever do find one I will go over hedge and ditch but what I will get to Him, for I will never finish without bringing in my master."

Perhaps you will think that I have gone a little over hedge and ditch, but I am persuaded that I have not, for the sixth verse comes in here, and brings our Lord in most sweetly, setting Him in the very forefront of you Bible readers, so that you must not think of reading without feeling that He is there who is Lord and Master of everything that you are reading, and who shall make these things precious to you if you realize Him in them. *If you do not find Jesus in the Scriptures they will be of small service to you,* for what did our Lord Himself say? "Ye search the Scriptures, for in them ye think ye have eternal life, but ye will not come unto me that ye might have life." Therefore your searching comes to nothing; you find no life and remain dead in your sins. May it not be so with us?

III. *Such Reading Is Profitable*

Lastly, such a reading of Scripture, as implies the understanding of and the entrance into its spiritual meaning, and the discovery of the divine Person who is the spiritual meaning, is profitable, for here our Lord says, "If ye had known what this meaneth, I will have mercy, and not sacrifice, ye would not have condemned the guiltless." It will save us from making a great many mistakes if we get to understand the Word of God, and among other good things we shall not condemn the guiltless.

I have no time to enlarge upon these benefits, but I will just say, putting all together, that *the diligent reading of the Word of God with the strong resolve to get at its meaning often begets spiritual life.* We are begotten by the Word of God: it is the instrumental means of regeneration. Therefore love your Bibles. Keep close to your Bibles. You who are seeking the Lord, your first business is to believe in the Lord Jesus Christ; but while you are yet in darkness and in gloom, love your Bibles and search them. Take them to bed with you, and when you wake up in the morning, if it is too early to go downstairs and disturb the house, get half an hour of reading upstairs. Say, "Lord, guide me to that text which shall bless me. Help me to understand how I, a poor sinner, can be reconciled to Thee." I recollect how, when I was seeking the Lord, I went to my Bible and to Baxter's *Call to the Unconverted* and to Alleine's *Alarm* and Doddridge's *Rise and Progress,* for I said in myself, "I am afraid that I shall be lost, but I will know the reason why. I am afraid I never shall find Christ, but it shall not be for want of looking for Him." That fear used to haunt me, but I said, "I will find Him if He is to be found. I will read. I will think." There was never a soul that did sincerely seek for Jesus in the Word but before long he stumbled on the precious truth that Christ was near at hand and did not want any looking for; that He was really there, only they, poor blind creatures, were in such a maze that they could not just then see Him. *Cling to Scripture. Scripture is not Christ, but it is the clue which will lead you to Him.* Follow its leadings faithfully.

When you have received regeneration and a new life, keep on reading, because it will comfort you. You will see more of what the Lord has done for you. You will learn that you are redeemed, adopted, saved, sanctified. *Half the errors in the world spring from people not reading their Bibles.* Would anybody think that the Lord could leave any one of His dear children to perish, if he read such a text as this: "I give unto my sheep eternal life, and they shall never perish, neither shall any pluck them out of my hand"? When I read that, I am sure of the final perseverance of the saints. Read, then, the Word and it will be much for your comfort.

It will be for your nourishment, too. It is your food as well as your life. Search it, and you will grow strong in the Lord and in the power of His might.

It will be for your guidance also. I am sure those go rightest who keep closest to the Book. Often when you do not know what to do, you will see a text leaping up out of the Book, and saying, "Follow me." I have seen a promise sometimes blaze out before my eyes, just as when an illuminated device shines out upon a public building. One touch and a sentence or a design flashes out. I have seen a text of Scripture flame forth in that way to my soul; I have known that it was God's word to me, and I have gone on my way rejoicing.

You will get a thousand helps out of that wondrous Book if you do but it; for, understanding the words more, you will prize it more, and, as you get older, the Book will grow with your growth, and turn out to be a grey-beard's manual of devotion, just as it was before a child's story book. Yes, it will always be a new book—just as new a Bible as if it was printed yesterday and nobody had ever seen a word of it till now; and yet it will be a deal more precious for all the memories which cluster round it. As we turn over its pages with delight do we recollect events in our history which will never be forgotten to all eternity, but will stand forever intertwined with gracious promises. The Lord teach us to read His book of life which He has opened before us here below so that we may read our titles clear in that other book of love which we have not seen as yet, but which will be opened at the last great day.

THE HOW AND WHY OF EFFECTIVE BIBLE STUDY

Dr. Wayne Mack

"From childhood you have known the holy Scriptures which are able to make you wise unto salvation through faith which is in Christ Jesus. All Scripture is inspired by God and is profitable for teaching, for reproof, for correction, for training in righteousness that the man of God may be adequate, thoroughly equipped for every good work" (2 Timothy 3:15-17).

"The Bible that is falling apart usually belongs to someone who isn't." In these words, Vance Havner speaks clearly to us about his conviction that a proper, regular study of the Bible is immensely profitable and practical. According to Havner, people who fall apart do so because they don't regularly and consistently study their Bibles.

C. H. Spurgeon affirmed his conviction about the incredible resource for living that is found in God's Word when he said, "If when I get to heaven the Lord shall say to me, 'Spurgeon, I want you to preach for all eternity.' I would reply, 'Lord, give me a Bible, that is all I need.'" Spurgeon believed that he had all he needed for preaching in the Bible because he was convinced that in the Scriptures we have all we need for successful living.

In chapter five of his book *How to Get the Most from God's Word,* John MacArthur emphasizes the importance and relevance of the Bible for our daily lives in this way. He writes:

> How important is the Bible to me? There are several ways to answer the question. Some say, "The Bible? It's just another book. It has some

> wise sayings here and there mixed with a lot of genealogies, myths and crazy visions."
>
> A second group says something like this: "Of course I know the Bible is important—at least my pastor thinks so. He's always quoting it and waving it in the air. But I don't read it much. I can't understand it too well."
>
> There is still a third group, however, who would align themselves with Sir Walter Scott, a famed British novelist and poet, who was also a committed Christian. On his deathbed Scott is reported to have said to his secretary, "Bring me the Book." His secretary thought of the thousands of books in Scott's library and inquired, "Dr. Scott, which book?" "*The* Book," replied Scott. "The Bible—the only book for a dying man."

John MacArthur then comments:

> And the committed Christian would have to add that the Bible is not just the only book for a dying man, but it's the only book for a living man, because it is the Word of God.[1]

It's evident from these statements that each of these men thinks highly of the practicality and profitability of Scripture for everyday living. Their statements reveal that they believe the Bible really does contain all the information we need for life and godliness. Well, were they right? Does the Bible, as Spurgeon declared, contain all the information that we need for time and eternity? Can, as Havner stated, a regular, consistent, careful, applicatory study of God's Word keep us from falling apart? Is the Bible, as MacArthur wrote, really the most important book for dying and living men? Are Spurgeon, Havner, and MacArthur overstating the case?

According to the apostle Paul, these men were absolutely right in their convictions about the comprehensive usefulness of Scripture. According to Paul, in the text quoted at the beginning of this chapter (and the rest of the writers of Scripture would have agreed with him), they were not overstating the case. "The Bible," writes Paul, "is able to make us adequate and thoroughly equip us for every good work" (2 Timothy 3:17). To be made adequate, according to *Webster's New World Dictionary*, means to be equal to a requirement or occasion, to be sufficient or suitable. So, Paul is telling us that through the Bible we can be made ready for and equal to any occasion, situation, or requirement. Now that's a powerful statement about the value of Scripture.

But that's not all Paul says to emphasize the practical usefulness of Scripture. He's not finished yet. In addition to making us adequate, he adds that the Scriptures can equip us for good works. And not just for some good works, but every good work. Put your mind in gear and think of any good work you can in your family, church, or society, and Paul would say that the Scriptures can equip you mentally, emotionally and behaviorally to do them. And more than that, he would want us to know that the Scriptures don't merely have the ability to equip us partially. No, Paul writes, they have the ability to equip us thoroughly for every good work. What a resource we have in God's Word!

When people read what Paul says about the comprehensive usefulness of God's Word, they might be inclined to ask several questions (I've heard all of these questions being asked by many people who are told about Paul's statement).

Why We Have Confidence in the Bible: Who Its Author Is

One question people ask is: "I hear what you're saying about the comprehensive value of Scripture. Why is the Bible able to do what you have stated it can do? Why do you have such confidence in its practicality?"

Numerous texts of Scripture indicate that we ought to be excited about the Bible because of the identity of its Author. "All Scripture is inspired by God" (2 Timothy 3:16). There is no other book in the entire world that has an author like this book. This book was given by inspiration of God.

What does it mean when the Bible says it was given by inspiration of God? Well, some think that it means that the men who gave us this book were inspired. You know, they were inspired in the same sense in which Beethoven may have been inspired to write a fine piece of music. Or they were inspired in the same way that Picasso or some other great artist may have been inspired to give us a painting that is out of the ordinary. Now it is true that the men who gave us this book were inspired. They were doing something out of the ordinary. They were out of the ordinary men. But that is not what the Bible means when it says it was given by inspiration of God. It does not simply mean that the men had an inspirational thought.

Others say that it means as we read the Bible, it is inspiring. You listen to a great piece of music and you come out and you are inspired, i.e., lifted up in your spirits, exuberant, moved emotionally. You see some dramatic scene and you begin to cry and you get emotionally moved and you are inspired to go out and do something or change your life in some way. And people say that is what it means when the Scripture says that it is inspired. It means when we come to it, we get inspired. We get challenged. That is true, but that is not what the text is saying.

Actually, the Greek word which is found here in 2 Timothy 3:16, translated "inspired by God," is a Greek word "theopneustos," which is a combination of two Greek words, "theos" and "pneustos." The Greek word "theos" means God, and the Greek word "pneustos" means breath. Really what the text is saying is that all Scripture is God-breathed! What does that mean? Well it means that Scripture has its origin in God. My breath doesn't come from outside of me. It is pumped out by my lungs, and whatever comes out of me is my breath. It has its origin in me. To say the Scriptures are God-breathed is the strongest possible way God could put it to indicate that what we have in this book is not simply the opinion of a man. What we have in this book is the very truth of Almighty God. It is inerrant, without error, infallible, all truth, altogether true and righteous, forever settled, absolutely trustworthy.

There is no other book like it. There is no other book in the entire world that you can read with the confidence with which you can read the Bible. Even books that were written by godly men in our day—good books—cannot compare with the Bible. As we read other books we need to compare them with the Scriptures to make sure that they really are sixteen ounces to the pound true. As we listen to a pastor preach, we need to search the Scriptures carefully to make sure that what he is saying is really according to the Word of God. However, when we read this book, the Bible, we can have absolute confidence that what we are receiving is absolutely true, without error, solid take-it-to-the-bank truth. It is God-breathed, given to us by a God who knows everything, who is all wise, who understands everything, who never needs to learn anything, who never needs to be counseled, who never needs to be given information from outside himself or by anyone else, who is never surprised by additional perspectives. These things never happen with God because, as God, He is altogether and comprehensively wise.

In general, the value that we place upon something is often related to the author or the producer of that something. Sometime ago I heard a story of a man who liked to visit antique shops. One day he went into an old antique shop and saw a dingy, dirty painting on the wall in that antique shop. It did not look like much, but he thought it had some potential. So he bought it. He paid thirty-five dollars for that painting. He took it home, varnished the frame and then worked on cleaning up the painting itself. Through his careful efforts, he was able to restore it to its original condition. He then hung it on his living room wall. Shortly after he had hung it on his living room wall a friend of his who was a connoisseur of art came to visit him. While sitting in this man's living room, he studied the painting on the wall and said, "Man, do you know what I think you have here?" "Yeah, I have a painting." "No, I think you have a painting by the famous Spanish painter, El Greco." The man who had purchased the painting said, "Do you really mean it?" "I think so, but I'm not an art expert, so let's take the painting to someone who is an art expert and have him look at it." They then brought the painting to someone who was an art expert. The art expert examined it and affirmed that really it was a painting by the famous Spanish painter, El Greco.

Guess what happened to the value of that painting at that point? Its recognized value immediately took a quantum leap. The man had bought that painting for thirty-five dollars, and a couple weeks later he sold the same painting for thirty-five thousand dollars. What changed the worth of that painting? It was the discovery of who the painter was. You see, I can paint something and it's not worth the price of the paper or the canvas it's painted on. In fact, because I'm such a poor and clumsy artist, the paper or canvas would be worth less after I had done some doodling on it than it was before I even touched it. No one would want to pay anything for it. No one would display it in their home or anywhere else. It would be good for nothing. It would quickly be thrown into a trash bin. But this is not so with a painting by El Greco or one of the other great painters of past or present history. The canvas on which these painters do their work isn't worth much, the paint isn't worth much, but because of their expertise and their skill, the painting is worth thousands of dollars, sometimes into the hundreds of thousands, even millions of dollars.

The fact that Scripture is God-breathed is what makes this book stand out from every other book. It is what gives this book its value. It's what makes this book comprehensively useful. It is why this book can make us adequate and thoroughly equip us for every good work. What we have in this book is truth that comes from Almighty God. That is why we ought to be excited about it. God has been pleased to reveal Himself in the Word. We can know something about God by viewing the heavens, for the heavens do declare the glory of God and the firmament shows forth His handiwork (Psalm 19:1). But if we want to know God fully, we must know Him in His Son, as He is revealed in Jesus Christ (John 1:18; 14:9; Hebrews 1:1-3), but even His Son has been revealed in the Bible (John 5:39; Hebrews 10:4,5). You don't find Jesus out in outer space. You do not find Jesus out in the creation. You find Jesus primarily in the Word of God. So, if we want to know God, if we want to know truth, if we want to know what is right and wrong, then we must turn to the Word of God. In the Bible, we have an absolute standard. We can come to this book with absolute confidence that whatever it says is right is right, and whatever it says is wrong is wrong. Because the Bible is God's Word, it is perfect, pure, right, clean, true and righteous altogether. And because it is God's Word, it is able to restore our inner man, cause us to rejoice, make us wise, clean us up, give us understanding and correct perceptions, bring pleasure, warn and protect us from danger, build us up, help us make wise decisions, change and transform us, make us truly prosperous and successful in the most important ways (John 17:17; Isaiah 8:19,20; Psalm 119:128; Psalm 19:7-11; Psalm 119:9-11, 105; Psalm 1:2,3; Joshua 1:8,9; Acts 20:32).

Why So Many Christians Are Poorly Equipped: Failure To Take The Medicine

When confronted with the concept of the comprehensive value of Scripture for all of life, another question people ask is: "If, as you say, the Scriptures can prepare us to handle any circumstance or occasion and thoroughly equip us for every good work, why is it that so many of Christians do not seem to be very prepared or thoroughly equipped?"

One answer to this question is that many Christians are not thoroughly equipped because they are not reading or studying or even hearing the Scriptures on a regular basis. Suppose I had a disease and there were a medicine to cure that disease. Suppose also that I didn't faithfully use that medicine. Whose fault would it be if my disease was not cured? Obviously, the fault would be mine. The medicine might be the best remedy in the world for solving my physical problem, but it would do me no good if I did not use it. No one in his right mind would fault the medicine for not solving my problem. No one would have any justification for complaining that the claims of the developer and provider were untrue or even exaggerated. The fact is, even good medicine does not work if it is sitting in a bottle in a medicine cabinet. It works when it is used regularly.

The same is true with the Scriptures. They prepare us for every circumstance and occasion and thoroughly equip us only when we use them. A Bible sitting on a shelf in a person's home or even carried with him wherever he goes does a person no good until he picks it up and reads it and studies it regularly. Most professing Christians have Bibles. Many of them have several Bibles, and sometimes they have several versions of Bibles. Truth is, these same professing Christians who claim to believe the Bible to be the Word of God—these same people who would agree that the Bible is to be our standard in matters of faith and practice—seldom, if ever, seriously read or study the Scriptures. These same professing Christians are sometimes people who do not attend a church where the Word of God is faithfully exposited and preached. They attend churches where they are entertained, but not edified, where the spiritual diet is not sound exegesis or solid theology, but cotton candy stuff with a little flavoring of Scripture. Or if they do attend a church where the Bible is exposited and preached, they are very sporadic in their attendance and thus they are not being consistently exposed to Biblical truth. Truth is, many professing Christians and churches are very flippant when it comes to their approach to the Scriptures. Whose fault is it that professing Christians are often not very well prepared and thoroughly equipped for every good work? The deficiency is not with the Bible; the deficiency is with people in their failure to use the Scriptures.

Many of us who call ourselves Christians do not realize the tremendous resources God has given to us in the Word of God. We say we believe the Bible, that it has everything we need for faith and practice; yet we do not act like we really believe that. When we have problems we fall apart, go to pieces and wonder what we are going to do and how we are going to get out of this. We do not have the confidence that God has given us what we need in His Word, and we do not turn to it for the help it can give.

In the light of the truth stated in 2 Timothy 3:17, it is amazing that so many who call themselves Christians really are not excited about this book. You can tell when people are not excited about this book because they do not read or study it! They can go for days without reading it, and if and when they do, they do it out of a sense of duty rather than delight. For them, Bible study is a chore. For them, there are many things they'd rather do than have devotions. Why? Because they don't understand what God has given them in this book.

Their attitudes and actions toward the Bible are not like the ones displayed by a teenage girl who came bouncing and bubbling into my office one day when I was a youth pastor in Park Ridge, Illinois. As she stood in front of me, excitement was written all over her face and expressed through her body language. Seeing this excitement, I tried to find out what had happened to make her this enthusiastic. I said to her, "Sharon, what are you so excited about?" She responded, "Wayne, it's tremendous!" I said, "Sharon, what's tremendous?" She said, "The Bible! It is so relevant! It is so practical. It is so helpful. It speaks to me just where I live."

If the Bible can do what 2 Timothy 3:17 says it can do, every Christian should be as excited about the Bible as Sharon was. Unfortunately, many are not. How do I know that? I know that because they neglect reading or studying or being present to hear it faithfully explained and taught. The result? They are not prepared for every circumstance they face in life, and they are not thoroughly equipped for every good work.

Why So Many Christians Are Poorly Equipped: Improper Use Of Scripture

A second reason why many Christians are not experiencing the wonderful reality of 2 Timothy 3:17 relates to their failure to use the Scriptures properly. It's possible to regularly read and study the Scriptures and still fall short of reaping the benefits described by Paul in this verse. In his second epistle, Peter tells us that it is possible to study the Bible and do so to our own destruction (2 Peter 3:16). In other words, Peter is talking about people who do read and study God's Word and then wrest, torture, and pervert the Scriptures. Obviously, these people were regularly reading Scripture — they could not be wresting, torturing or perverting God's Word if they were not reading it and, at least, had some acquaintance with the words found in it.

Well, how were they wresting the Scriptures? Probably in several ways. For one thing, it's possible to torture the Scriptures by making them say and mean what God never intended them to say or mean. It is also possible to torture the Bible by emphasizing certain truths to the neglect of other truths. As you examine earlier portions of 2 Peter, it seems evident that there were some who were so emphasizing the doctrine of Divine Sovereignty, easy believism, and an incorrect understanding of salvation by grace that they were neglecting the doctrine of human responsibility, the importance of personal effort, the necessity of perseverance, and the importance of developing and increasing Christian character qualities in the lives of Christians (See 2 Peter 1:2-11).

From 2 Peter 1:12-21, it would appear that there were people who were putting more confidence in personal experience and "cunningly devised fables" — made up stories — than they were in the truth found in Scripture. Scripture and history inform us that there were people who lived in the time of Peter who would take a word or phrase from Scripture and then build some fanciful and unrelated teaching on it. They would do something similar to what "Bible code" people do in our day. They would look for hidden and secret teaching that had nothing to do with the historical, cultural, or grammatical context or purpose of the passage on which they supposedly built their fanciful interpretations. Paul calls these people "word wranglers." He calls their teaching "empty and worldly chatter" (2 Timothy 2:14-16). He says that they "pay attention to myths and endless genealogies," that they are given to "mere speculations," that they have turned aside to "fruitless discussion," and that they are teaching "strange doctrines" (1 Timothy 1:3-6).

In chapter two of 2 Peter, Peter deals more specifically with people who secretly bring in what he calls "damnable heresies" — distortions or perversions of the truth. These people misinterpret the Scriptures and make them say what they want them to say rather than what God intends them to mean. They twist the meaning of God's Word so that it will be to their own liking and advantage, so that it will make them look and feel good, so that it will support their ideas and opinions, so that it will allow them to live as they want to live and do what they want to do and still consider themselves good Christians.

To derive the benefit of 2 Timothy 3:17 out of Bible reading and Bible study, certain practices must be employed and others avoided. We must have a balanced approach to our study of Scripture. We must avoid the practice of overemphasizing certain aspects of Scripture and completely ignoring others. We must never use the cafeteria system of Bible study, taking what we like and rejecting what we don't like. We must shun the practice of eisegesis (reading our own ideas into Scripture) rather than exegesis (drawing out of the Scripture what is really there, letting the Bible speak for itself). We must not read into the Scriptures what we want to be there. Instead, we should let the Scriptures speak for themselves. We must steer clear of bringing our views to the Scripture and making the Bible conform to our preconceived ideas. Our concern should be to bring out of the Scriptures what God has put into them. We must not lift biblical sentences out of their context, but make sure we are interpreting them in keeping with the immediate context in which they are found and in keeping with the larger context of the rest of God's Word.

We ought to learn about the historical and cultural context of the book we are studying and avoid being superficial and overly subjective in our attempt to understand Scripture and make it relevant. Before we draw out applications for ourselves and others, we should labor to comprehend the situation of the people to which the texts of Scripture were originally addressed. We must not overlook the importance of the tenses of the verbs that are used in our interpretive attempts. To rightly understand and apply Scripture, we should seek to define biblical words by comparing Scripture with Scripture and devote ourselves to discovering God's purpose for including the passage we are studying in His Word. The ultimate issue is not what do I think the passage is saying or what does it mean to me, but what does God mean in this passage, what did it mean to its original readers and what purpose did God have in mind when He chose to include it in His Word. Unless we follow these simple interpretive rules, we are not ready to make application of the passage to our own lives and situation and we will not derive the maximum 2 Timothy 3:17 benefit out of our Bible study.

The distorters of whom Peter was speaking in 2 Peter 3:16 were violating these simple rules to the extreme. To some people, these distorters may have appeared to be basing their views on Scripture. They may have even quoted Bible verses and used Bible words, but, according to Peter, they were misusing the Scriptures. In reality, though they may have given the semblance of being biblical, they were not, in the words of Paul in 2 Timothy 2:15, "accurately handling the Word of Truth." And as a result, they were promoting their own destruction and the destruction of anyone who would listen to them. According to Peter and Paul, people who do this kind of thing with Scripture are torturing the Scripture and therefore not deriving the benefit that a right understanding and application of God's Word can bring.

As mentioned in the last paragraph, these distorters were involved in serious and extremely destructive distortion of God's Word. Their study and teaching of the Word had a very negative effect on themselves and others. Others, including you and me, may not distort God's Word to the extent that these men did and therefore the destruction we experience and wreak on others may not be as obvious. The consequences of our inaccurate handling of the Bible may be much more subtle. It may manifest itself by stifling the positive and explosive impact that we, and others whom we may influence, could be deriving from Scripture. It may manifest itself in our lack of preparation for the various situations and occasions we face in life.

Why So Many Christians Are Poorly Equipped: Low Regard For Scripture

A third answer to the question, "If, as you say, the Scriptures can prepare us to handle any circumstance or occasion and thoroughly equip us for every good work, why is it that so many Christians do not seem to be very prepared or thoroughly equipped?" is related to or an extension of what we have just noted in answer two. However, this answer is so important that I want to give it special attention all by itself. The third main reason why 2 Timothy 3:17 is not more of a reality in the lives of many Christians is that they do not regard and use the Scriptures in the way that 2 Timothy 3:16 says it should be regarded and used. They may, on occasion, read Scripture, even study the Scriptures, even hear the Scriptures being taught, but they do not enter into a consideration of the Bible with the focus of 2 Timothy 3:16.

This great text tells us that "All Scripture is inspired by God and is profitable…" To really benefit from Scripture we must come to it with the attitude that we will profit from our study. There are some people who do not believe the Bible is valuable at all. People like Madeline Murray O'Hare and others in the past and present want to destroy the Bible. They think it has no place in our school systems and any other public place. They believe the Bible is impeding our progress as people. They do not think studying the Bible has any value, but that it is harmful and hurtful.

Other people would not go that far; they would not say studying the Bible is of no value. They might say, "Yes, the Bible is valuable, it is profitable; it is profitable to learn about ancient history." After all, there are some ancient civilizations that are described more clearly and fully in the Word of God than any place else. So people study the Bible to learn about ancient civilizations—about the Horites, the Hittites, and the Jebusites. These people may pore over the pages of the Word of God to find out about ancient civilizations. There are non-believers who spend hours, even years studying the Bible as an ancient history book. These people say it is valuable to learn about ancient history, but that is not what Paul had in mind when he said, "All Scripture is profitable."

There are other people who think the Bible is profitable for learning about Bible doctrine. So these people come to God's Word primarily to learn facts and information about various theological points. They study to be able to prove the biblical nature of their theological convictions so they can show people where they are wrong. When somebody challenges them about Bible doctrine, they go back and pore through the Scripture for support of their perspective and then go out and argue with other people. These people seem to think that the Bible is primarily valuable to win theological arguments.

I know of people who seem to study the Bible primarily for that reason. They love to study the Bible to learn Bible doctrine. They can talk to you about the hypostatic union of the two natures of Jesus Christ; they can talk to you about superlapsarianism and infralapsarianism, double predestination, the ordo salutis and other intellectual-sounding theological points. On various issues, they have amassed their texts from the Word of God to prove their points or to disprove the points of others. Primarily their approach to the Scriptures is a very doctrinal kind of approach. 2 Timothy 3:16 makes it very clear that this is not the primary purpose for which God gave us His Word.

Now, please do not misunderstand me. I think we ought to know about Bible doctrine, but that is not the primary purpose for which God gave us His Scripture. And because some people study and teach the Bible in this way, many professing Christians find the Bible dry, dull, and boring. They hear Sunday School teachers and pastors who communicate the idea that the Bible's exclusive purpose is to teach abstract theology. As people hear the Bible taught in this way again and again, they come away saying, "So what? How does it relate to my life?" I remember going to hear a very well known preacher. This preacher preached for about forty-five minutes expounding some great Bible doctrine in an academic, scholastic fashion. Then he stopped without helping us to understand how that great doctrine applied to our daily lives. When I came out of that meeting I said to my wife, "So what? He never helped us to understand how that great doctrine applied to our lives. He said nothing that would make anyone think that it had any relevance to us right here and now." In the message, there was no application to my life. I was not shown how it related to me or what my response should be. On that occasion I said to my wife, "That kind of preaching is why many people are not interested in preaching, why many people are not interested in the Bible."

Well, the Bible was never given merely to teach us abstract doctrine. Paul says in 2 Timothy 3:16, "all Scripture is inspired by God and is profitable…" Then he goes on to tell us what it is profitable for, and as he does this, he is telling us how we must view and use our Bibles if we are to become equipped for every good work. These are the things you should have in mind as you hear a message from the Word of God and as you read the Bible. To really benefit from God's Word you must study it to be taught, reproved, corrected, and trained in righteousness.

One Thing You Must Do To Really Benefit From Scripture: Be Teachable

To really benefit from Scripture, you must come to the Bible with the realization that it "is profitable for teaching." You must come with willingness and a desire to be taught. You must come as a student, with the attitude of a learner. Now, that presumes we do not know much. It presumes that we are ignorant. And indeed we are! Scripture says that our foolish minds are darkened (Ephesians 4:17). We think we are so smart. We think we are so wise. But in reality, we are very stupid. We need to come to this Book to find out what is true. Do you realize that you do not know ultimate truth by discovery? Nobody discovers ultimate truth. You know truth by revelation. If you know ultimate truth, it is because God has been pleased to reveal it to you and He has revealed it in the Word (1 Corinthians 2:1-14).

The truth of the matter about ultimate truth is that unless you know everything, you cannot know anything. Let me illustrate. Here are these four blind men and as they are walking along they bump into something, but do not know exactly what it is. The one guy puts his arms around a part of the something he bumped into and says, "It's the trunk of the tree." A second man grabs hold of a part of the something he bumped into and says, "It's a rope." A third blind man grabs a hold of a part of the something he bumped into and says, "It's a fire hose." The fourth blind person grabs hold of a part of the something he bumped into and says, "It's the side of a barn."

All four of these blind men bumped into the same elephant. Yet, one of them says it is a fire hose, another says it is a rope, another says it is the trunk of a tree, and another says it is the side of a barn. How can it be that they all described this same elephant so differently? This happened because each of them encountered and felt only a part of the elephant. If each of them had encountered the whole of that elephant, they would have had a different understanding of what they were encountering and would have described and identified it differently.

Similarly, we have a lot of people who are trying to describe truth and yet they describe and define it so differently. One of them says this is the truth, someone else says something else is the truth, someone else says, "You guys are wrong – this is the way it is," and on and on it goes with each person claiming to have the truth, but describing it differently. One news reporter for *U.S. News and World*

Report described the situation well when he wrote about a convention of 8,000 psychologists that met in Phoenix, Arizona. In this article he described the various views of these people who were recognized as experts in understanding people and their problems. After observing and listening to the discussions, he drew this conclusion, "All of the experts are here and none of them agree."

Why are there so many versions of the truth? Why do not the experts agree? Several answers could be given to this question, but certainly one of them must be: they don't agree because all of them see only a part of the picture, only a part of reality. In keeping with our elephant illustration, the experts do not agree because they do not see all of the elephant and indeed cannot see all of the elephant because of their finiteness. The truth is such that unless you see all of reality you cannot know anything for sure because what you do not know may completely change your understanding of what you do know. The truth is, there is only One who knows everything. There is only One who knows what happened from eternity past and who knows what will happen to eternity future. There is only One who knows things perfectly and absolutely, and that is God! It follows then that since God is the only One who knows everything, He is the only One who really knows anything about ultimate truth. What this means is that if we want to know anything for sure, we need to hear the truth from the One who knows everything. Fortunately for us, the One who knows everything has given us the truth in His Word (Psalm 19:9; John 17:17). If we want to know truth, we need to come to the Word as learners, as people who have open and eager minds, as people who desire to learn from the One who knows everything.

If we want to know about God, here is where we find the truth about God. If we want to know about hell, we will not get together a group of knowledgeable people and say, "What do you think about hell?" No, the wisest of men only see a part of the picture. We need to come to the Word of God and let God tell us about hell. If we want to know about life after death, we will not read what Kubler-Ross wrote in her books about death and dying or what Dr. Moody wrote in his book, "Life after Life." These people are only finite. If we want to know what really happens after death, we need to come to the Word of God. If we want to know about salvation, how a man gets right with God, we will not gather together a group of people and ask them, "What do you think?" Rather, we should come to the Word of God given by inspiration of God because God, who knows everything, really knows how a man is to be saved.

If we want to know how we should conduct our marriages or raise our children, we should not go to a group of secular marriage counselors or psychiatrists or psychologists and ask them what they think. They do not know everything. What they have to say is only their opinion. If we really want to know the truth, we are not going to put our confidence in some fallible, finite men. We are going to put our confidence in God. God knows how to rear my children, so we are going to believe what He has to say. If we want to know about business ethics and principles, and/or about the way we as employers or employees should function, we will not get together a group of business experts and say, "What do you think?" No, God in His Word has much to say about Christians and their work (business) life. The book of Proverbs and many other passages of Scripture are replete with practical truths about business. Why did God include these truths in His Word? Because they are profitable for teaching us about the work and business aspects of our lives.

The Bible is profitable for teaching. Question: for teaching about what? Stated positively, the answer is: The Bible is able to teach us "everything that pertains to life and godliness" (2 Peter 1:3). It is able to teach us everything we need to make us "adequate and thoroughly equipped for every good work" (2 Timothy 3:17). Stated in negative fashion, the answer is: There is no area of life for which the Bible does not contain important truths that will help us in our relationship with God and people—important truths about the past, present, and future. If words mean anything, we must approach our Bible study with the attitude that "everything" is comprehensive. It means "everything." This means that if we want to reap the benefits of 2 Timothy 3:17 and 2 Peter 1:3, we must come to our Bible study as a student with a humble, receptive, submissive attitude and an insatiable desire to be taught.

A Second Thing You Must Do To Really Benefit From Scripture: Welcome Reproof

To really benefit from Scripture in the 2 Timothy 3:17 way, you must come to the Bible with the realization that it "is profitable ... for reproof." The word "reprove" and the concept of "reproving" does not rank at the top of what people want done to them or want to do to others. On a hit list of profitable things, the word and concept of reproof probably would not even appear. Truth is, most of us do not like to be reproved. We just do not think of reproving as something that is beneficial or profitable. When I was a child I never liked to be reproved by my dad. I would just as soon escape that benefit. I did not want it and did not like it when Dad did it to me. There are many of us as adults who still think and act like children when it comes to reproof. We just do not like to be told that what we are doing is wrong. We would much rather have somebody tell us what is right about us and how wonderful and how neat we are than have somebody come up to us, like Nathan did with David, and stick their long, scrawny finger under our nose and say, "You are the man! What you have done is wrong. You need to acknowledge your sin and change." But God knows that even though we do not like reproof, it is good for us. So He gave us this Book and uses it to reprove us because He knows that being rightly reproved is good for us.

Being rightly reproved is a major step in becoming adequate and thoroughly equipped for every good work. I have personally experienced it in my own life when people have used the Word to reprove me. I have also observed the benefit of reproof in the lives of others as I have counseled them. For example, a few years ago, a couple who was having serious problems in their marriage and family life came to me for counseling. The man was huge—very tall (six feet, five inches) and very muscular (well built, probably 260 to 270 pounds of muscle). He looked like he could have been a lineman for some professional football team. His wife was much shorter and thinner. In fact, she looked somewhat fragile. I noticed that her hair was unkempt, disheveled, even matted. Her face was black and blue; her eyes were just about swelled shut. As she sat there, she would not even lift up her eyes to look at me, but sat in my office staring at the floor, acting like a nervous, fidgety, scared rabbit.

In the course of counseling them as I attempted to understand this woman (how she thought, what she valued, what was going on in her life), I said to this woman who seemed so beaten down, "Tell me, what do you like to do, what do you enjoy? What are some of your abilities? What are some of the things that you've accomplished in life? What are some of the things that you feel good about?" She hung her head and finally said, "There are two things that I like to do and feel good about. Number one, I went to beautician school and I like to work as a beautician." (I could hardly believe what I heard her say. In the light of the way her hair was, or perhaps I should say was not, fixed and the way she was dressed, it was not what I would have expected her to say.) She continued, "I like being a beautician and I think I am good at it." After she said that, her husband jumped in and began to criticize her saying, "Yes, but..." and then went on to make some negative, put-down remarks. Included in these remarks was some information about his wife's excessive drinking and her failures as a wife and mother. When he finished, I said to the woman, "OK you like to be a beautician. What is the next thing you like to do and have some ability to do?" She said, "Well, I like to play the piano." And then she started to talk about the joy she got out of playing the piano. At that point, her husband again jumped in and said, "Yes, but...." and then went on to make some more negative, put-down remarks.

When he did this for the second time, I calmly and yet firmly said to him, "John (this was not his real name), your wife is wrong. She is failing to fulfill her responsibilities. She has sinfully responded to her environment. She has turned to the bottle for relief rather than turning to God. She has withdrawn from life. She has wasted the gifts that God has given to her. She is not living for Jesus Christ as she ought. She is wrong. She is sinning. But I want to tell you something, John, you are sinning also." (I knew he was sinning against her because I could see the evidence of his beating his wife on her face, and previously I had heard him calling his wife derogatory names and screaming at her.) "You have provided the environment in which she has responded in these sinful ways. You are not encouraging your wife, you are not loving her as Christ loved the church. You are not loving her as you love yourself. You are not nourishing her. You are not cherishing her as the Bible says you should. Instead, you have mistreated and abused your wife. You are not fulfilling God's commands for you as a husband as found in Ephesians 5:25-31 and 1 Peter 3:7. God is not pleased with the way you are treating your wife. John, you are sinning against God, and you need to repent of your sins. You need to seek forgiveness from God and your wife."

I said all of that calmly and without yelling. I said it as gently as I could, but I did say it with force. As I was talking, I could see John's face getting red and redder. I saw him clenching his fists. I saw his body becoming tenser. I wondered what he would do, how he might respond to me. I had seen what he had done to his wife's face. When he did not like something she said or did, he used her face as a punching bag. The thought flickered through my mind that my face might be the next face to be used in the same way. When I finished, John got up and started storming back and forth in my office. As he paced, he was ranting and raving and fuming, "You are not going to talk to me that way, nobody talks to me that way, and nobody gets away with it." I thought he was coming toward me and I shot off a prayer. Suddenly, John turned and headed for the door. In my mind's eye I can still see John going through the door, and I can still hear the words he spoke as he left my office: "I'm going to pray that God burns this place down." And he was gone. I think it is fair to say he was angry. He did not like what I said. He despised being reproved.

Two weeks after that event, I was sitting in my study when there was a knock on the door. I said, "Come in." When the door opened, I saw big John standing there. I wondered if he had come back to finish what he had not finished previously. On the previous occasion, he had assaulted me verbally, but was he now going to vent his anger on me physically? He walked into my office, stood in front of my desk and moved nervously from one foot to the other. He hung his head, looked a little sheepish and said, "Dr. Mack, you know what happened two weeks ago." "Yes, I remember." (How could I forget?) "You know how angry I became?" I said, "Yes, I remember." He said, "I want to tell you why. I became angry because you were telling me the truth, and I didn't want to hear it."

Did I enjoy reproving John? No! Did John enjoy receiving that reproof? No! Should I have reproved John? Yes! Was that biblical reproof profitable for John? Yes! It was the beginning of real change in his life and in the life of his family. They began to attend counseling and both made professions of faith. And for the first time in their marriage they became involved in a local church, where they could fellowship with other believers and hear the Word of God faithfully preached. Biblical reproof was beneficial for John.

It was part of God's process of making him adequate and thoroughly equipped for every good work.

Big John needed that and so do you and I. To experience the benefits described in 2 Timothy 3:17, we need to be shown where we are sinning. We need to be rebuked. We need God to take His sword of His Spirit and grind it into the depths of our heart. We need God to take the searchlight of His Word and search out the nooks and crannies of our hearts.

As Hebrews 4:12 states, God's Word is quick and powerful, piercing even to the dividing asunder of the soul and spirit and is a divider of the joints and marrow. It brings to light the sinfulness of our thoughts and motives. It constructively and necessarily criticizes us. And we do need God to criticize us. We do need God to rebuke us. We do need God to show us where we are wrong. All of this is beneficial because, you see, the beginning of improvement is understanding where you are wrong. If I am sick, the beginning of getting well is to discover what is wrong with me. I go to the physician, not to have him tell me, " Let us see… your fingernails seem to be doing real well, and your skin seems to be covering up your flesh real well." I do not go to him to have him tell me what is right about me. I go to the physician to have him poke around and tell me what is wrong with me. Why? It is when he discovers what is wrong with me that we can do something about it.

We ought to come to God's Word with the same attitude. When we come to our personal study of this Book or to a Bible study group or to a church service or to biblical counseling, we ought to come saying, "O God, today show me what is wrong with me. Lord, show me where I am in error. Lord, show me where I am failing. Lord, show me where I need to improve." We ought to do this because when we approach Scripture in this way, we are using it in the way God intended it to be used. After all, He's the One who said that Scripture is profitable for reproof.

In Proverbs 15 God expands on this thought that reproof is beneficial in the last two verses of the chapter. Proverbs 15:31 tells us at least two things about the value of godly reproof. One, it tells us that godly reproof is life giving. In these words, God is saying, "Do you really want to live life with a capital L?" If so, you will need to be reproved. If you really want life, you will have to be reproved. Still further, the same verse informs us that being rightly reproved is a fundamental requirement for becoming wise. If you refuse to listen to reproof, God says you'll never become truly wise. Moreover, Proverbs 15:32 tells us that if you avoid reproof you are despising yourself. In other words, when you refuse the right kind of reproof, you are hurting yourself, destroying yourself, preventing yourself from experiencing the benefits of 2 Timothy 3:17.

A Third Thing You Must Do To Really Benefit From Scripture: Accept Correction

To really benefit from Scripture in the 2 Timothy 3:17 way, you must also come to the Bible with the realization that it "is profitable...for correction...." Isn't that great? The Bible doesn't just knock us down. The Bible is not like those thieves described by Jesus in Luke 10:30. In this passage, our Lord Jesus Christ tells us of what happened to a certain man when he was walking along the road from Jerusalem to Jericho. As he traveled along, some thieves who were hiding behind some boulders accosted him. They jumped out from behind those boulders, knocked him down, beat him, stripped him, took his money and then left him lying there on the ground bleeding and dying. They did not care. They wanted to hurt and wound him and then leave him on the ground to die.

The Bible is not like that. Yes, a proper usage of the Scripture will strip us of our pride, of our self-righteousness, of our sin, but it does not just strip us. Yes, when rightly used, it will wound us through its reproofs, but it does not merely wound us. Yes, when rightly used it will knock us down, but it won't merely knock us down. This same Book that God uses to reprove us will also pick us up, put us on our feet, dust us off, head us in the right direction, and tell us how to straighten out the crooked places in our lives.

Think back to the "big John" illustration. John was having serious problems in his life and marriage, no doubt about it. What did he need? He needed to be taught what a good marriage ought to be, what he should be as a husband. Where would he find the information he needed about these issues? In the Book inspired by the One who knows all things, the originator of the marriage institution. He needed to know what God had to say about having a good marriage, about being a good husband. Then, having learned from God's Word what a good husband ought to be, he needed to be taught where and how he was failing. He needed to learn in specifics where and how he was not being the husband that God wants him to be. He needed to be shown his sin and experience conviction of that sin. He needed life-giving reproof. But what instrument should be used to bring him under conviction? Again, the answer is the Bible because in it, an all-wise, all-knowing God shows us how we are failing.

John, however, needed more than teaching and more than reproof. He also needed instruction on how to correct the wrongs in his life and in his marriage. Where could John go to find infallible, inerrant information about the right thing to do to untangle the mess he had created, to learn what changes he should make, and what actions would be constructive and appropriate? What John did not need at this point was the fallible ideas or opinions, the guesswork of men. He needed to be sure that what he did to correct the situation was solid gold, take-it-to-the-bank directions that would be pleasing in the sight of the God to whom he was accountable and constructive in repairing his own life and marriage. Where could John get that kind of direction? Only one place! In the Book inspired by the God who is the great Corrector, the great Repairer, the great Restorer, and the great Transformer.

I could give many illustrations of the corrective ministry of the Bible, but will mention only one more. A certain man, a Christian who was a dentist, came for counseling after his wife had left him for another man. As he sat in my office, he spilled out the whole story to me. Then he said, "What should I do?" I said, "I'm not going to give you my opinion because my opinion isn't any better than anyone else's. I'm going to tell you what I'm convinced God wants you to do." I knew, because he had told me, that others had been saying, "Forget about her. She's not worthy of your love. She's not worthy of being with you. She ran off with another man. Let her go. Good riddance to bad rubbage." I said, "Do you really want to know what God wants you to do?" After he responded in the affirmative, I said, "From what you've told me, it seems clear that your wife has grievously sinned against God and you. However, I suspect that there are probably some ways in which you have failed in your husbandly responsibilities. She's not here, so I can't talk to her, and it will do us little good to spend our time talking about her. Matthew chapter 7:2-5 tells us that when we have a problem with another human being we should begin by looking at our own sins and failures, and only after we've done that are we ready to consider the other person's sins and failures. As hard as that may be, I'm convinced that's where God would have you start in this situation. Are you willing to do that? Do you really want to handle this situation in a God-ordained way?" Again, he responded in the affirmative. So I said, "Let's look at the Bible and see what the Bible has to say about you as a husband and your responsibilities, and let's seek to find out if there are ways in which you have failed in your God-given responsibilities." We then began to look at several relevant passages of Scripture about how a husband should treat his wife and live with her.

In the course of our initial counseling sessions, I would have him read a verse or passage of Scripture and then I would ask him, "What do you think God means by this statement we have just read? How does that apply to you? If your wife were here, what would she say about the way you have been fulfilling this biblical responsibility?" He would then attempt to answer my questions and I would follow with affirmation, correction, amplification, expansion, illustration, and application. Again and again, after looking at a passage of Scripture, I would hear him say, "I didn't do that, I didn't do that. I wasn't treating my wife the way God wanted me to treat her. I was inconsiderate and thoughtless, selfish and unloving, etc. I'm guilty of not being the husband I should have been." As we worked our way through the Scripture, God used His Word to teach and reprove this man. Never once did I hear him defending or excusing himself. Never once did I hear him justifying his neglect. God pierced this man's heart and he freely acknowledged his sin.

At this point in the counseling, I said to him, "You've acknowledged your sins to yourself and me. If you're serious about wanting to deal with this situation God's way, there are others to whom you must yet confess your sins and ask for forgiveness." I followed that statement with an explanation that his failure to obey God's Word was a sin against God as well as his wife and that he needed to confess his sin to God and his wife. I next asked him, "Are you willing to do this?" He assured me that he was and so I gave him some further instructions about how to do this and then said, "When you confess your sins to your wife, I don't know how she will respond. I don't know what will happen. I don't know if she will laugh at you for doing this. I don't know if she'll just say, 'You're right, you have been a miserable husband, but now it's too late. I've already made up my mind that it's over. I'm not coming back to you.' But, Jim (not his real name) regardless of what she does, this is what I'm convinced God would have you do." I gave him instructions about how to make up his "log list" (using the husband's log list in *A*

Homework Manual for Biblical Living, Volume 2 as a template) and what to say when he approached his wife.

In all of this, I believe I was giving him counsel based on Scripture. This man went out to follow through on what we had discussed. A few days later, my telephone rang and a woman on the other end of the line said, "I am Dr. so and so's wife. I understand he's been coming to you for counseling. I would like to know if I could come with him to the next appointment." He had done something that she had never heard him do before. He had specifically confessed and asked for forgiveness. Well, God used that to impact the woman, and now she wanted to come for counseling. The two of them entered into counseling, during which we used the Bible to teach, reprove and correct. The marriage was put back together again. They continued to come for counseling and do the biblical homework I assigned for a number of weeks. God turned that marriage around, and they left counseling experiencing a joy in marriage the likes of which they had never had before. Through the Scriptures, both of them were made adequate for the marriage situation.

Primarily, the examples I have used to illustrate the usefulness of Scripture have related to marriage, but please do not make the mistake of thinking that is the only area in which they are useful. No, the right use of the Scriptures can make us adequate and thoroughly equip us for every good work. During the more than fifty years I have been a Christian, I have personally benefited from the teaching, reproving and correcting ministry of God's Word hundreds of times and in every aspect of my life. During the more than forty years in which I have been ministering to people, I have literally counseled thousands of people who had all sorts of very serious problems other than marriage and family problems. What did these people need? They needed to be made adequate and thoroughly equipped for every situation. How would this be facilitated? Through biblical teaching, biblical reproof, and biblical correction. In this ministry, I have again and again directed them to the teachings, reproof and correction of God's Word for what they needed. And again and again I have found that the Bible provided just what was required.

A Fourth Thing You Must Do To Really Benefit From Scripture: Start Training

To really benefit from Scripture in the 2 Timothy 3:17 way, you must also come to the Bible with the realization that it "is profitable ... for training in righteousness."

"You can't teach an old dog new tricks." "That is just the way I am." "I was born that way." "That is the way my parents were." "I'm just like my mother, or I'm just like my dad." These are statements people often make when they are confronted with the need for change. I have heard all of these statements, again and again. I have heard these statements from people who were challenged to change and become better husbands. I have heard these statements from women who were challenged to be better wives. I have heard these statements from parents who were challenged to be more godly parents, or children who were challenged to be more godly children. I have heard these statements from people who were challenged to be more sensitive, more considerate, and more loving. I have heard them from people who were challenged to be more industrious, more organized, more zealous, more disciplined. I have heard them from people who were challenged to be more appreciative, more expressive, more positive, and less critical. I have heard them from people who were challenged to use their anger properly or to control their appetite or their lusts. I have heard them from people who were challenged to be more truthful or more cheerful.

When people make these statements, they think the case is closed. They think that once they have said, "You cannot teach an old dog new tricks" or have made any of the aforementioned statements, there's nothing more to be said." They are convinced that these statements must represent the truth because they and others think this way and say these things.

Actually, what needs to be said to these people is that none of these statements is true. The Bible, which is true and righteous altogether (Psalm 19:9), says they are not true. God, who knows everything and cannot lie, says they are not true. For that matter, God in His Word says the very opposite. He says, "You can be 'trained for righteousness.'" His Word indicates that you and I can change regardless of what our mother and father may have been. We can be different even if we were trained for unrighteousness from birth. From birth we may have developed habit patterns that were sinful and unproductive, but the good news is that those of us who are united to Christ through repentance and faith can be retrained so that our habit patterns of thinking, acting, and reacting are righteous before God. The good news is that we do not have to continue to blow it again and again. The good news is that we don't have to be habituated to doing it the wrong way. We can be trained to do it the right way (God's way). For years, we may have thought and lived the wrong way, but through the proper use of the Scripture, we can become adequate and thoroughly equipped to perform good works in any and every situation.

In Ephesians 4:17, Paul says to Christians, "Don't walk anymore as the Gentiles walk." The word "walk" implies that we had a particular lifestyle, certain habitual ways of thinking and living. In particular, we had a lifestyle, a manner of life like that of the Gentiles. The word "gentiles" is another word for unbelievers, for people who are not Christians. So, Paul says, "At one time our habitual manner of life (our thoughts, words, actions, desires, reactions, standards, values) was just like other unbelievers." "Now," he says (Ephesians 4:17-24), "you have become Christians, you have learned Jesus Christ, you are being renewed in the Spirit of your minds, and you must no longer walk that way.

Now, you must and can put off your ungodly habit patterns and lifestyles (manners of life), and you must and can put on godly habit patterns and lifestyles (manners of life). You were trained to live unrighteously, but since you are a new creation in Christ, you can get rid of your old manner of life and be retrained for righteousness."

This same truth is sounded out by Paul in 1 Timothy 4:7, where he commands us to train ourselves for the purpose of godliness. Note carefully what he says and suggests in this text. First he suggests that before we became Christians we had an ungodly manner of life. Second, he suggests that even though we have become Christians, we carry over into the Christian life some ungodly habit patterns. Third, he does not indicate that we should just accept our ungodliness and continue to live with it because there is nothing we can do to change these patterns. Fourth, he indicates that we can develop a manner of life that is oriented toward godliness. And fifth, this change will not come automatically. It will be accomplished through training in which we will actively, not passively, be involved. New, righteous habit patterns can be developed. Again, Paul is making it clear that even though we have been trained to develop ungodly manners of life, we can through proper training develop godly lifestyles.

At this point, the question we should be asking is, "Yes, but how? How is this marvelous change facilitated? How do we put off ungodly, unrighteous manners of life and develop righteous, godly manners of life?" Second Corinthians 3:18 and many other passages indicate that this transformation is accomplished through the work of the Spirit (Galatians 5:16, 22, 23, 25; Philippians 2:13; Romans 8:1-13). Romans 12:2 and Ephesians 4:23 teach that God accomplishes this change through the renewing of our minds. The mind in Scripture is a synonym for heart. It includes our thought processes, our affections, our desires and motivations, our values, everything the Bible means when it speaks of the inner man (2 Corinthians 4:16; Ephesians 3:16,17). So this change facilitated by the Holy Spirit involves developing a new mind, i.e., developing new ways of thinking, feeling, new desires and motivations, new values and aspirations. This change occurs as the Holy Spirit trains us to develop new inner man patterns. It happens as He helps us to develop a renewed mind.

But the question still remains: How does the Holy Spirit accomplish this change? What does He use to train us in this righteousness? Second Timothy 3:16 provides the clear and unmistakable answer to this questions. The Scriptures are "profitable for... training in righteousness." On a practical level, the instrument the Holy Spirit uses to train us in (to habituate us to) a lifestyle of righteousness is always the Scriptures. He does not do this with a holy zap. He does not do this primarily through general revelation. He does not do this through the Koran or any other so called holy book. He does not do this through the writings of philosophers, psychologists, or psychiatrists. He does not do this through visions or dreams or ecstatic experiences. He is irrevocably and everlastingly committed to making this transformation happen through the proper use of Scripture. Second Timothy 3:16 established that fact in an irrefutable way.

But that brings up another question: What does this training involve? The answer again is obvious. It is found in the meaning of the Greek word found in the last phrase of 2 Timothy 3:16. The Greek word used here is "paideia," which was used to describe what parents were supposed to do for their children. They were to bring them up by means of training that involved instruction and discipline. And this training was something that would require active, continuous, consistent, regular effort over a long period of time. Good child training was not done in a day, nor was it done sporadically. It was a daily task that required being consistent in instruction and discipline.

The English word "training" conveys the same idea. Webster defines training in terms of bringing up or rearing, disciplining or making proficient, preparing or making fit. As illustrations of what training involves, he mentions the process used to prepare people to be nurses or to play sports or to make an animal behave in a particular way. The clear inference of the English word is that training requires active, continuous, consistent, regular effort over a long period of time.

Implicit in these definitions is the concept that training involves preparing someone to function in a particular and desirable way on a regular basis. Implicit is the idea that through training old habits will be replaced with new and better habits.

In particular, as applied to the teaching of 2 Timothy 3:17, Paul is telling us that becoming adequate and thoroughly equipped for every good work will involve training. If you are a pastor who has unique responsibilities and challenges as a leader of God's people or if you are a layperson who faces all sorts of challenges in life, you can experience these benefits only as you are regularly and consistently taught, reproved, corrected, and trained in righteousness by the Word of God. You must, Paul would have us know, approach the Scriptures with a desire to have these four things happen. You must come to the Scriptures with the proper attitude – the attitude of a learner, wanting to be taught; the attitude of humility, wanting to be reproved; the attitude of faith, looking for correction and following through with the corrective directions it gives; and the attitude of a disciple, wanting to be trained and knowing that you will be trained only if you come to the Scriptures regularly, consistently, and continuously.

This brings us full circle to the comments from Havner, Spurgeon and MacArthur at the beginning of the chapter. Havner believed that "The Bible that is falling apart usually belongs to someone who isn't," because he believed the truth of 2 Timothy 3:16,17. Spurgeon believed that the Scriptures were all he needed because of the truth of this passage. And MacArthur believed that the Bible is the only book for a dying or living man because of the truth declared in 2 Timothy 3:16,17.

Now, what about you? Will you believe the truth of 2 Timothy 3:16 and use your Bible for the purposes and in the way taught by this passage? If you will and do, you will experience the benefit of 2 Timothy 3:17.

Suggestions For Getting The Maximum Benefit From This Chapter:

A. Reread this chapter, and as you do use a highlighter pen to highlight the most important statements that are made in this chapter.

B. Write out your answer to the following questions:

1. What reasons do Christians have for believing that the Bible is the most reliable book in the entire world?
2. What reasons do Christians have for believing that the Bible is the most helpful book in the entire world?
3. Why are many professing Christians so ill-equipped to handle the inevitable challenges and problems of life?
4. Why do you think many professing Christians spend so little time studying Scripture?
5. How did people torture or wrest the Scriptures in the time of the early church?
6. How do people today torture or wrest the Scriptures? What have you observed in this regard? How have you twisted or misused the Scripture?
7. What important rules must we keep in mind if we are to accurately handle God's Word?
8. What has God been teaching you from His Word in recent days?
9. In what areas has God been using His Word to reprove you in recent days or in the past?
10. In what areas has God been using His Word to correct you in recent days or in the past?

11. In what areas has God been using His Word to train you in righteousness in recent days?
12. In what areas do you need to become more adequate and more thoroughly equipped for good works?
13. In the light of the material presented in this chapter, what changes do you need to make in your life in terms of the way you personally study or listen to God's Word?

Bible Study

Session No. 1

A. How would you rate the importance of reading or studying the Bible? Check one or more.

1. Absolutely essential and should be done regularly. _____

2. Very desirable and should be done frequently. _____

3. All right if you have time. _____

4. When you really have a problem, it's a good time to turn to the Bible. _____

5. Makes no difference -- it is up to the individual. _____

6. Other opinion than those already stated. _____

B. Make a list of reasons for answering the previous question as you did. Support your reasons with Scripture.

1. ____

____

2. ____

____

3. ________________________________

   ____

4. ________________________________

   ____

5. ________________________________

   ____

6. ________________________________

   ____

7. ________________________________

   ____

8. ________________________________

   ____

9. ________________________________

   ____

10. ________________________________

    ____

C. Study the following verses and note the attitude they reflect toward reading or studying the Bible.

1. According to Job 23:12, how would Job have answered the question posed in Section A?

____

____

Write out how Job expressed his view of the importance of God's Word.

____

____

2. According to Psalm 119:72, 82, 92, 116, 127, how would the Psalmist have answered the question?

____

____

Write out how the Psalmist expressed his view of the importance of God's Word.

Verse 72 ________________________________

Verse 82 ________________________________

Verse 92 ________________________________

Verse 116 _______________________________

Verse 127 _______________________________

____

3. According to Jeremiah 15:16, how do you think Jeremiah would have answered the same question?

____

____

What did Jeremiah say that leads you to this conclusion?

____

____

____

4. According to Matthew 4:4, Mark 12:24, and John 15:7, how do you think Jesus Christ would have answered the same question?

____

____

Write out how Jesus Christ expressed His view of the importance of God's Word.

Matthew 4:4 ________________________________

____

Mark 12:24 ________________________________

____

John 15:7 ______________________________

____

5. According to 1 Peter 2:2, how do you think Peter would have answered the same question?

____

____

What did Peter say that leads you to this conclusion?

____

____

6. According to Colossians 3:16 and 2 Timothy 2:15, how do you think Paul would have answered the same question?

____

____

Write down what Paul said that leads you to this conclusion.

____

____

Colossians 3:16 ______________________________

____

2 Timothy 2:15 ______________________________

____

D. Study the following verses to discover some reasons for regularly reading and studying God's Word. Note especially what the **Word** is and what it does.

1. John 20:31

   a. ______________________________

   b. ______________________________

   c. ______________________________

2. John 5:39-40; 1 Peter 1:23; Romans 1:16

   a. ______________________________

   b. ______________________________

   d. ______________________________

3. 2 Timothy 3:13-17

   a. ______________________________

   b. ______________________________

   c. ______________________________

   d. ______________________________

   e. ______________________________

   f. ______________________________

g. ______________________________

h. ______________________________

i. ______________________________

4. 1 Peter 2:2; Acts 20:32; John 17:17; James 1:21

a. ______________________________

b. ______________________________

c. ______________________________

d. ______________________________

e. ______________________________

5. Hebrews 4:12; Jeremiah 23:29; John 15:3; Ephesians 5:26

a. ______________________________

b. ______________________________

c. ______________________________

d. ______________________________

e. ______________________________

f. ______________________________

6. Romans 15:4

   a. ______________________________

   b. ______________________________

   c. ______________________________

7. Hebrews 5:14; John 12:48

   a. ______________________________

   b. ______________________________

E. List the personal insights or challenges you have received through this study. How should your attitude toward and use of the Bible be different? Be personal and specific.

   1. ______________________________

   2. ______________________________

   3. ______________________________

   4. ______________________________

   5. ______________________________

   6. ______________________________

   7. ______________________________

   8. ______________________________

Bible Study

Session No. 2

A. Study the following passages and notice what Jesus Christ did with the Bible. Write down what you discover.

1. Luke 4:16-21

   a. ____________________

   b. ____________________

   c. ____________________

   d. ____________________

   e. ____________________

2. Matthew 5:17; 21:5

   a. ____________________

   b. ____________________

3. Luke 18:31-33

   a. ____________________

   b. ____________________

4. Luke 24:27

   a. ____________________

   b. ____________________

5. Matthew 4:1-14

   a. ______________________________

   b. ______________________________

   c. ______________________________

   d. ______________________________

6. Matthew 22:29-32

   a. ______________________________

   b. ______________________________

   c. ______________________________

7. Matthew 21:6-17

   a. ______________________________

   b. ______________________________

   c. ______________________________

   d. ______________________________

8. Matthew 19:3-5

   a. ______________________________

   b. ______________________________

9. Matthew 26:51-54

   a. ______________________________

   b. ______________________________

10. John 3:14; Matthew 12:40; Luke 17:26-27

   a. ______________________________

   b. ______________________________

   c. ______________________________

   d. ______________________________

   e. ______________________________

   f. ______________________________

   g. ______________________________

B. Study the following verses in Psalm 119 and write down what the Psalmist did with the Word of God.

1. Psalm 119:11 ______________________

2. Psalm 119:13 ______________________

3. Psalm 119:14 ______________________

4. Psalm 119:22, 56 ___________________

5. Psalm 119:23, 48, 97, 99 ______________

6. Psalm 119:30 ______________________

7. Psalm 119:43,74,81 ____________________

8. Psalm 119:45 ____________________

9. Psalm 119:51 ____________________

10. Psalm 119:59 ____________________

11. Psalm 119:66 ____________________

12. Psalm 119:69 ____________________

13. Psalm 119:92 ____________________

14. Psalm 119:95 ____________________

15. Psalm 119:104, 105 ____________________

16. Psalm 119:120 ____________________

17. Psalm 119:128 ____________________

18. Psalm 119:161 ____________________

C. Consider and write down what the following verses teach us to do with our Bibles. Note any benefits mentioned in connection with obeying these directives. Think carefully about what each directive means. (Not all passages mention the benefits specifically. Where the benefit is mentioned, write it down. Where it is not, leave a blank.)

1. Joshua 1:8, 9

Directive Benefit

a. ____________________

b. ____

c. ____

2. Psalm 1:2, 3

Directive Benefit

a. ____

b. ____

c. ____

3. Ezra 7:10

Directive Benefit

a. ____

b. ____

c. ____

4. Deuteronomy 6:6-9

Directive Benefit

a. ____

b. ____

c. ____

d. ____

e. ____

f. ______________________________

5. Deuteronomy 4:2

Directive Benefit

a. ______________________________

b. ______________________________

c. ______________________________

6. Deuteronomy 11:18

Directive Benefit

a. ______________________________

b. ______________________________

7. Proverbs 6:20-23

Directive Benefit

a. ______________________________

b. ______________________________

c. ______________________________

d. ______________________________

8. Isaiah 8:19, 20

Directive Benefit

a. ____

b. ____

9. Isaiah 34:16

Directive Benefit

a. ____

b. ____

c. ____

10. Luke 11:28

Directive Benefit

a. ____

b. ____

11. John 2:22

Directive Benefit

a. ____

b. ____

c. ____

12. John 8:31; 15:7

Directive	Benefit

a. ______________________________

b. ______________________________

13. Acts 17:11

Directive	Benefit

a. ______________________________

b. ______________________________

c. ______________________________

14. Ephesians 6:17; 1 Thessalonians 2:13

Directive	Benefit

a. ______________________________

b. ______________________________

15. Colossians 3:16

Directive	Benefit

a. ______________________________

b. ______________________________

16. 2 Thessalonians 2:15; 2 Timothy 1:13

Directive	Benefit

a. ______________________________

b. ______________________________

c. ______________________________

17. 2 Timothy 3:15; 2:15

Directive	Benefit

a. ______________________________

b. ______________________________

c. ______________________________

18. 2 Timothy 4:2-5

Directive	Benefit

a. ______________________________

b. ______________________________

c. ______________________________

19. James 1:21-25

Directive	Benefit

a. ______________________________

b. ______________________________

c. ______________________________

d. ______________________________

20. 1 Peter 2:2; 2 Peter 3:1,2; Jude 17

Directive	Benefit

a. ______________________________

b. ______________________________

21. 1 Timothy 4:13; Revelation 1:3

Directive	Benefit

a. ______________________________

b. ______________________________

c. ______________________________

D. Evaluate your use of the Bible in the light of this Bible study. Identify areas of neglect and seek to make the necessary corrections. How should your use of the Bible be changed?

1. ______________________________

2. ______________________________

3. ______________________________

4. ______________________________

5. ____________________________________

6. ____________________________________

7. ____________________________________

Bible Study

Session No. 3

A. A person who has only recently become a Christian approaches you for help in getting more out of the Bible. He says, "I really want to profit from my Bible study, but I don't know how to go about it. Would you give me some suggestions to guide me?" What suggestions would you give him? (Charles Spurgeon's sermon on "How to Read the Bible" will be helpful in answering this person.)

1. ______________________________

2. ______________________________

3. ______________________________

4. ______________________________

5. ______________________________

6. ______________________________

7. ______________________________

8. ______________________________

9. ______________________________

10. ______________________________

11. ______________________________

12. ______________________________

13. ______________________________

14. ______________________________

B. How could you use the following verses in giving help to the aforementioned person? How do they relate to Bible reading or Bible study?

1. John 3:3 ______________________________

____

2. 1 Corinthians 2:10-14 ______________________________

____

3. Psalm 119:18; Ephesians 1:17; Colossians 1:9 ______

____

4. Deuteronomy 17:19, 20 ______________________________

____

5. Psalm 1:2 ______________________________

____

6. Mark 1:35; Daniel 6:10 ______________________________

____

7. Luke 24:25-27; John 5:39 ______________________________

____

8. 2 Timothy 3:16, 17 (According to these verses, what are five of the purposes of Bible study?)

   a. ______________________________

   b. ______________________________

   c. ______________________________

   d. ______________________________

   e. ______________________________

9. Acts 17:11 (Notice at least five things that the Bereans did with the Scriptures.)

   a. ______________________________

   b. ______________________________

   c. ______________________________

   d. ______________________________

   e. ______________________________

10. Isaiah 66:2 ______________________________

    ____

11. John 17:17; Acts 10:33; James 1:21-25; Matthew 7:24-28

    a. ______________________________

    b. ______________________________

c. ______________________________

d. ______________________________

e. ______________________________

12. Romans 3:12 ______________________________

____

13. Habakkuk 2:2; 2 Peter 3:15, 16 ______________________________

____

14. 1 Timothy 4:13; 2 Timothy 2:1-5; Proverbs 2:1-5

____

15. Acts 8:30, 31; Nehemiah 8:8; Ephesians 4:11, 12

____

16. Nehemiah 9:3 ______________________________

____

17. 1 Thessalonians 1:5-8 ______________________________

____

C. Make a list of personal insights or challenges you have received through this study. Be specific. How should your attitude or approach to Bible study be changed or improved?

1. ______________________________

2. ______________________________

3. ______________________________

4. ______________________________

5. ______________________________

6. ______________________________

7. ______________________________

8. ______________________________

9. ______________________________

10. ______________________________

Bible Study

Session No. 4

A. Give all the reasons you can think of as to why Christians neglect Bible study or Bible reading.

1. ______________________________
2. ______________________________
3. ______________________________
4. ______________________________
5. ______________________________
6. ______________________________
7. ______________________________
8. ______________________________

B. Identify the problems you have in your Bible reading or Bible study. How can the problems be solved?

1. ______________________________
2. ______________________________
3. ______________________________
4. ______________________________
5. ______________________________

6. ______________________________

C. Evaluate the statements:

"I don't need to go to church to have some preacher explain the Bible to me. I have the Holy Spirit in me to help me interpret the Bible for myself." Or, "I don't ever read Commentaries or 'Christian' literature about the Bible. I don't need any human help in understanding the Bible. I get all the help I need from the Holy Spirit." How would you reply to these statements?

1. ______________________________

2. ______________________________

3. ______________________________

4. ______________________________

5. ______________________________

6. ______________________________

D. Study the following Scripture verses and note what they indicate about the use of human help in studying the Bible.

1. Acts 8:30, 31 ______________________

____

2. Matthew 28:18-20 ____________________

____

3. 2 Timothy 4:2-5 ______________________________

____

4. Acts 17:11 ________________________________

____

5. 2 Timothy 4:13 _____________________________

____

6. 2 John 9-11 _______________________________

____

7. 2 Corinthians 2:17; 4:1,2 ___________________

____

8. 1 John 2:20, 27 ____________________________

____

E. What would you say to a person who asserts, “I’ve tried to read my Bible, but actually I never have been able to understand it. It just doesn’t make sense to me. Besides that, I find Bible reading very boring, so I’ve stopped even trying to read it. I’m sure I can be just as good a Christian without reading my Bible. I know of people who read their Bible and go to church all the time who don’t seem to be any better for it”? (To answer this question, keep in mind the Scripture we have considered in the preceding studies. J. C. Ryle's sermon on Bible reading will also be helpful.)

1. ______________________________

2. ______________________________

3. ______________________________

4. ______________________________

5. ______________________________

6. ______________________________

7. ______________________________

8. ______________________________

9. ______________________________

F. Make a list of the insights and challenges you have received from this Bible study. Be specific and personal. What changes or improvements should you make in your Bible reading and Bible study practices?

1. ______________________________

2. ______________________________

3. ______________________________

4. ______________________________

5. ______________________________

6. ______________________________

7. ______________________________

8. ______________________________

9. ______________________________

10. ______________________________

Bible Study

Session No. 5

A. Consider the charge that since the Bible was completed almost two thousand years ago, it is irrelevant for us today. One man said to me, "The world has changed. People have changed. You can't apply a first-century Bible to a twentieth-century world."

1. How would you answer this charge? What would you say to this man? How would you demonstrate the relevancy of the Bible? (J. C. Ryle's sermon on Bible reading will be helpful in showing the constant relevancy of the Bible.)

   a. ______________________________

   b. ______________________________

   c. ______________________________

   d. ______________________________

   e. ______________________________

   f. ______________________________

   g. ______________________________

   h. ______________________________

   i. ______________________________

2. Why do some people have this opinion?

 a. ______________________________

 b. ______________________________

 c. ______________________________

 d. ______________________________

 e. ______________________________

 f. ______________________________

 g. ______________________________

 h. ______________________________

B. Many religious sects such as the Mormons and Christian Science claim that they do respect the Bible but assert that they have received additional and even superior revelations from God. Others, who are not members of these sects, also declare that they have been given fresh revelation from God. Look up the following verses and note how they answer these claims.

1. Jude 3 ______________________________

 ____

2. 2 Timothy 3:13-17 ______________________________

 a. ______________________________

 b. ______________________________

c. ______________________________

d. ______________________________

3. 2 John 9 ______________________________

____

4. Colossians 2:6-10 ______________________________

____

5. Galatians 1:6-9 ______________________________

____

6. John 17:20 ______________________________

____

7. Hebrews 1:1-3 ______________________________

____

8. Hebrews 2:1-4 ______________________________

____

9. 2 Timothy 2:15-18 ______________________________

____

10. 1 Timothy 6:3-6 ______________________________

____

11. Ephesians 2:20 ______________________________

____

C. Make a list of "mistakes" to avoid in Bible reading or Bible study. (A review of the Scripture in session 3, section B, and session 4, section D, will be helpful in formulating this list.)

1. Don't be guilty of picking and choosing what truths of Scripture you will believe or read or put into practice (Acts 10:33; 2 Timothy 3:16).

2. Don't study the Bible merely to satisfy your intellect or to help you win an argument. Rather study the Bible to know God and Christ better and to be changed by what you learn. Seek to apply the Scripture specifically and personally (Psalm 119:105; 2 Timothy 3:16, 17; Matthew 28:19, 20; Luke 11:28; Revelation 1:3).

3. ____

____

4. ____

____

5. ____

____

6. ____

____

7. ______________________________

   ____

8. ______________________________

   ____

9. ______________________________

   ____

10. ______________________________

    ____

11. ______________________________

    ____

12. ______________________________

    ____

D. Make a list of tools that will be helpful for Bible study. (Some are essential; others are optional, but helpful.)

   1. A good, clear, readable, accurate translation of the Bible.

   2. One or two other versions of the Bible for checking out difficult passages.

   3. ______________________________

   4. ______________________________

5. ______________________________

6. ______________________________

7. ______________________________

8. ______________________________

9. ______________________________

10. ______________________________

E. Describe the procedure you follow in your Bible study.

1. ______________________________

2. ______________________________

3. ______________________________

4. ______________________________

5. ______________________________

6. ______________________________

7. ______________________________

F. Ask a radiant, growing Christian to describe his Bible study procedure.

1. ______________________________

2. ______________________________

3. ______________________________

4. ______________________________

5. ______________________________

6. ______________________________

7. ______________________________

8. ______________________________

9. ______________________________

G. List the insights and challenges you have received from this study. Be personal and specific.

1. ______________________________

2. ______________________________

3. ______________________________

4. ______________________________

5. ______________________________

6. ______________________________

7. ______________________________

Bible Study

Session No. 6

A. What should be our goals as we study a passage of Scripture?

1. To understand what the Holy Spirit means in the passage. This will require observation, meditation, and interpretation.

2. To discern what changes the Holy Spirit wants to make in our lives through the passage. What is He saying in this passage to us? How does this passage reprove us? How does it correct us? How does it train us in righteousness? How does it equip us for good works?

3. To actually implement the passage in our daily lives. This will involve specific planning and application, immediate and purposed action, and personal examination and review. Scripture says, "But prove yourselves doers of the Word and not merely hearers who delude themselves" (James 1:22).

4. ______________________________

____

____

5. ______________________________

____

____

6. ______________________________________

____

____

B. One Proven Method of Bible Study.

1. *Select the passage of Scripture to be studied.* Generally speaking, the passage should be part of a book of the Bible which you have chosen to read consecutively. You should not form the habit of jumping all over the Bible, simply studying passages by chance or that happen to be familiar or appealing to you. The Holy Spirit wrote the Bible as He did because He wants us to study it in context and consecutively. Occasionally, the "hop, skip, and jump" method or a topical, doctrinal study involving many passages may be a legitimate diversion, but the usual practice should be the consecutive reading of a book.

   New converts and Bible students may want to study the Gospel of Mark and other shorter or relatively simpler books of the Bible before tackling some of the more difficult and larger books (2 Peter 3:15, 16). However, since "all Scripture is given by inspiration of God and is profitable," no part of the Scripture may be neglected. Some record of Scripture read and studied ought to be kept and consulted to insure a proper balance in our spiritual diet. Some Christians have exposed themselves to the varied aspects of God's truth:

   a. By reading from an Old Testament book in the morning and a New Testament book in the evening.

b. Or by reading and studying a book in the Old and New Testament alternatively.

c. Or by reading a portion from the Old and New Testament during the same Bible study session.

2. Having selected the passage to be studied, *ask God to help you understand, apply, and obey His Word.* Keep in mind such Scripture as Psalm 119:18; Ephesians 1:17; 1 Corinthians 2:12-14; Colossians 1:9; and 1 Samuel 3:9.

3. *Read the passage that you have chosen for the day.* You may find it helpful to *read it out loud.* The message will then come through the ear gate as well as the eye gate. You may also want to read it in two or three versions. *Read the passage slowly and distinctly,* seeking to really understand what is being said. Try to picture in your mind the action, the concepts, and the meaning of the passage.

4. Go back over the passage and make mental or written notes of the facts. Try the following passage as an example—Matthew 1:18-25.

   a. This is how Jesus was born.

   b. Mary was betrothed to Joseph, but before they were married she was found to be an expectant mother through the influence of the Holy Spirit.

   c. Joseph, her betrothed husband, was an upright man who did not want to disgrace her. So he decided to divorce her secretly.

(Now you take over and record the remaining facts of the passage.)

d. ______________________________

____

e. ______________________________

____

f. ______________________________

____

g. ______________________________

____

5. Consider and record the interpretation or meaning of the above facts:

   a. Jesus Christ was supernaturally conceived.

   b. God brought His Son into the world in a most unusual way.

   c. Things are not always as they appear to be.

   d. Joseph was a righteous man, yet he was merciful and gracious.

   (Now you take over.)

   e. ______________________________

   f. ______________________________

g. ______________________________

h. ______________________________

(For the time being, either bypass the portions that puzzle you or note what puzzles you and ask your pastor or consult a commentary. "The Bible," said Augustine, "is like a great river, it is deep enough for an elephant to swim in but shallow enough for a child to wade in." Do not worry about passages that are mysterious. You may not understand them now, but at a later date, as you appropriate what you do understand, God may even help you to understand the more difficult passages. Meanwhile, do not be discouraged or confused.)

6. Consider and record what specific applications this passage has for you. Ask and answer: What does the truth of this passage mean in my life? How should this truth affect the way I live? What specific changes do I need to make?

   a. I must be willing to believe that God can do the impossible.

   b. I must recognize that God sometimes does things in a way we don't expect.

   c. I must be slow to judge and condemn until I am sure I have all the facts.

   d. I must stand up for the truth, for righteousness, but I must also be gracious and merciful.

   (All of these applications will become even more challenging and life transforming if made more specific by examining my life to see when I didn't do what they indicate or when I did do what they indicate. For example, application "c" would really have some bite if I would ask, When did I judge and condemn without the facts or when didn't I condemn or judge before I had the facts?)

(Now you take over.)

e. ____

____

f. ____

____

g. ____

____

h. ____

____

i. ____

____

j. ____

____

7. Turn what you have learned into prayer.

    a. *Thank God* for opening His truth to you in a practical way.

b. *Confess your sin* as it has been opened to you by this passage.

c. *Ask God for forgiveness,* for further understanding, and for the help of the Holy Spirit to put the truths you have learned into practice. Be very specific.

8. As you go on your way:

a. *Reflect* on what God has spoken to you through this passage (Psalm 1:2).

b. *Make deliberate application* in specific situations.

c. *Share* what God has taught you with someone else within twenty-four hours.

d. *Review* your life during the past twenty-four hours to see when you have and when you have not implemented the truths you have learned.

C. List the insights and challenges you have received through this study. Be personal and specific.

1. ____________________

2. ____________________

3. ____________________

4. ____________________

5. ____________________

6. ____

7. ____

8. ____

9. ____

D. Select the book of the Bible you will study and begin to use the method we have discussed in this assignment.

   1. What book of the Bible will you study? __________

   2. When will you begin? ________________________

   3. With whom will you share the results of your study?

      ____

Bible Study

Session No. 7

In this concluding session, two other methods of Bible study are described. You will want to experiment with these methods by completing the example studies that are included and then by launching out on your own. If this manual is used for group studies, an entire session may be devoted to each method.

A. The Question and Answer Method.

1. Follow steps 1 through 3 mentioned in session 6, section B.

2. Break the passage down into paragraphs or sections of thought. Give each section a descriptive title. (The *New Berkeley Version* of the Bible arranges the content of the Bible in paragraphs. The *New American Standard* Bible designates paragraphs by bold-face numbers or letters.)

   Example: Mark 2:1-28

   Descriptive titles for sections of thought.

   a. Mark 2:1-12: Man through the roof.

   b. Mark 2:13-17 ______________________________

   c. Mark 2:18-22 ______________________________

   d. Mark 2:23-28 ______________________________

3. Study the individual sections of thought in your passage and write down your answers to various questions.

   When studying a narrative or historical portion of the Scripture such as the Gospels or the book of Acts, the following questions may be helpful.

   Example: Mark 2:1-12

   a. *Who* is mentioned?

      (1) ______________________________

      (2) ______________________________

      (3) ______________________________

      (4) ______________________________

      (5) ______________________________

   b. *What* actually happened?

      (1) ______________________________

      (2) ______________________________

      (3) ______________________________

      (4) ______________________________

      (5) ______________________________

      (6) ______________________________

(7) ______________________________

(8) ______________________________

(9) ______________________________

(10) ______________________________

c. *Where* and *when* did this incident take place? (Sometimes this will be recorded and important to understanding and applying the passage. At other times the time and place are neither mentioned nor important.)

(1) ______________________________

(2) ______________________________

(3) ______________________________

(4) ______________________________

(5) ______________________________

(6) ______________________________

d. *Why* did this incident take place?

(1) The fame of Jesus was spreading swiftly (Mark 1:45).

(2) Jesus was presenting His messianic credentials (Matthew 11:2-5; Isaiah 35:5-6).

(3) ______________________________

(4) ______________________________

(5) ______________________________

(6) ______________________________

e. *What* is God teaching me in this passage?

(1) Jesus is the Messiah of God, who fulfills all the messianic prophecies of the Old Testament.

(2) ______________________________

(3) ______________________________

(4) ______________________________

(5) ______________________________

(6) ______________________________

(7) ______________________________

(8) ______________________________

(9) ______________________________

(10) ______________________________

f. *What* personal, specific challenges does this passage bring to me? What difference should the truths of this passage make in the way I live? What sins do I need to confess? What changes do I need to make? What do I need to commit to God in prayer?

(1) I need to realize more fully the tremendous power of Jesus Christ.

(2) I need to change my attitude toward affliction. I need to see that affliction may be the means by which God brings me and others into contact with Jesus Christ, teaches us great wisdom, and displays His glory (Psalm 119:71; Mark 2:12; John 9:3).

(3) ______________________________

____

(4) ______________________________

____

(5) ______________________________

____

(6) ______________________________

____

(7) ______________________________

____

(8) ______________________________

____

4. Other questions which may be used with almost any passage of Scripture are:

a. What does this passage teach me about God? About Jesus Christ? About the Holy Spirit?

____

____

b. What is the main point of the passage?

____

____

c. Why did the Holy Spirit include it in the Bible? What does He want to do with it?

____

____

d. What doctrinal truths are taught in this passage?

____

____

e. What commands or exhortations are found in this passage? Are they commands or exhortations I need to obey?

____

____

f. Are any errors, sins, or problems mentioned? Are these errors, sins, or problems found in my life? What must I do to correct these things?

____

____

g. What comfort, encouragement, or promises are found? Are they for me? Do I have a right to be consoled by them?

____

____

h. Are there any examples in the passage which I should follow?

____

____

i. Is there anything in the passage I do not understand? Whom should I ask or where should I look for help?

____

____

j. Are there any other Scripture passages which are quite similar that will help me to understand this passage? (Use your concordance or center references to discover these passages.)

____

____

k. What has God taught me from this passage? What sins do I need to confess? What changes do I need to make? What do I need to ask, praise, or commit to God in prayer? With whom will I share what I have learned? (Select a passage and experiment with these questions. Why not try Mark chapter 1?)

____

____

(Specific, helpful questions on every chapter in the Bible are found in *Search the Scriptures,* a book published by Inter-Varsity Press. The questions in this book may be used with great profit. A brief introduction to every book of the Bible is also provided.)

5. Conclude your Bible study by following steps 7 and 8 mentioned in session 6, section B.

B. The Discovery Method of Bible Study.

1. Follow the procedure described in steps 1 and 2 of session 6, section B.

2. Begin reading the Scripture and continue until you find a portion of Scripture that has some special significance to you.

3. Write down the Bible reference, the promise, the command, the challenge, the phrase, the idea that captures your attention.

4. *Think about your selection.* Check cross-references or look up specific words in a dictionary or concordance. Think of opposite or similar words. Seek to make specific applications to your life. Write down the pith of your thoughts. Especially record the reason that particular section was of such significance to you.

5. *Turn to God in prayer.* Thank Him for the message He gave you. Ask Him to help you profit from it and live by it.

6. *Carry the thought with you throughout the day.* Meditate on it as often as you can. Share what God has taught you with someone else.

7. *Begin your next Bible study session where you finished this study.* Go through the same procedure again. Read until God gives you something for your heart and life.

8. *Example of the Discovery Method*

    a. Choose to read 1 Thessalonians.

    b. Seek God's help in prayer. "Lord have mercy on me. I want to love you and your people more. I lack insight and understanding of your Word. You have said that you wouldn't suffer the soul of the righteous to famish and that the hand of the diligent maketh rich (Proverbs 10:3, 4). Make me rich in spiritual things. Help me to be diligent. Open your Word to me. Come, Good Shepherd, help me to know you. I don't want to be a spiritual dwarf. Speak to me, for Jesus' sake. Amen."

c. Begin reading in chapter 1 and read until some portion captures your attention.

(1) Perhaps you might be challenged by the way Paul and his friends gave thanks for the Thessalonian Christians in verses 2 and 3. If so, you would stop there and do the things mentioned in the summary of the Discovery Method. You would want to consider and notice that they gave thanks for all the Christians, that they gave thanks in prayer, that they gave thanks to God, that they gave thanks always, that they gave thanks for the Thessalonians' work of faith, labor of love, and steadfastness of hope in our Lord Jesus Christ, and that they let the Thessalonians know they appreciated them.

(2) Or perhaps you would not be gripped until you read through verse 7. Perhaps, because of your particular circumstances or needs, you would be particularly challenged by the way the Christians of Thessalonica had been an example to other believers. If so, you would pause at this point and do the remainder of things mentioned in the preceding summary of the Discovery Method.

APPENDIX

Helpful Books:

Matthew Henry's Commentary on the Whole Bible, by Matthew Henry, Sovereign Grace Publishers.

One Volume Commentary on the Whole Bible, by Jamieson, Fausset, and Brown, Associated Publishers and Authors, Inc.

The Treasury of Scriptural Knowledge, by Canne, Browne, Blayney, Scott, and others, Revell Co.

Crudens Concordance, by Alexander Cruden, Revell Co.

Zondervans Pictorial Dictionary of the Bible, ed. Merril C. Tenney, Zondervan Publishing House.

The New Bible Commentary, ed. F. Davidson, Eerdmans Publishing Co.

Search the Scriptures, ed. Alan M. Stibbs, InterVarsity Press.

Psalm 119, by Charles Bridges. The Banner of Truth Trust.

Young's Analytical Concordance of the Bible, by Robert Young, Eerdmans Publishing Co.

Talks About the Bible, by Ernest F. Kevan, Walter Ltd.

Profiting From the Word, by A. W. Pink, The Banner of Truth Trust.

Interpretation of the Scriptures, by A. W. Pink, Baker Book House.

The Divine Inspiration of the Bible, by A. W. Pink, Reiner Publications.

Thy Word Is Truth, by Edward Young, Eerdmans Publishing Co.

Fundamentalism and the Word of God, by J. I. Packer, Eerdmans Publishing Co.

The Way, chapter 3, by Godfrey Robinson and Stephen F. Winward, Moody Press.

Tyndale Old Testament and New Testament Commentaries, various authors, Eerdmans Publishing Co.

Helpful Tapes:

Words of Life Tape Library, 110 Old State Rd., Media, Pa. 19063, has thousands of tapes containing expositions of the Bible. These tapes are available on a loan or purchase basis. A catalog of available tapes may be secured by sending $1.00 to the address mentioned above.

Tapes numbered 975 and 976 are studies by J. I. Packer on the Place and Function of the Scriptures in the Life of the Church and the Christian.

Tape number 331 is by Ian Tait and is titled *The Peace, Place and Power of the Bible.*

Tapes numbered 1030-1039 contain a reading of the whole Old Testament.

Tapes numbered 1198-1203 contain a reading of the entire New Testament.

ENDNOTES

[1] John MacArthur, *How To Get the Most From God's Word* (Dallas: Word Publishing, 1997), 47.